THE CARETAKER OF ALL SOULS

An Intimate Interview with Death

CRISTINA CARBALLO-PERELMAN, M.D.

Copyright 2015

ISBN: 978-0-9967412-6-2

Library of Congress Control Number: 2015918243

Printed in the United States of America

First Edition

Publisher: CCP Enterprises, LLC

Cover Design: Sebastian Carballo

ALL RIGHTS RESERVED. NO PART OF THIS PUBLICATION MAY BE REPRODUCED OR TRANSMITTED IN ANY FORM OR BY ANY MEANS—ELECTRONIC OR MECHANICAL—INCLUDING PHOTOCOPYING, RECORDING OR VIA ANY INFORMATION STORAGE RETRIEVAL SYSTEM WITHOUT PERMISSION IN WRITING FROM THE COPYRIGHT OWNER.

TABLE OF CONTENTS

Dedication v

Forward vi

Introduction vii

PART 1: MEDICAL TRAINING AND BEYOND 1

Chapter 1: Medical School—The Early Experiences 1
Chapter 2: Residency and Fellowship—Continuing Early Experiences 21
Chapter 3: Life Experiences as an Attending Physician 46

PART 2: DEATH'S HISTORY 59

Chapter 1: The Cultural Perspective 59
Chapter 2: The Afterlife 64

PART 3: THE MANY FACES OF DEATH 73

Chapter 1: Suicide 73
Chapter 2: Euthanasia 80
Chapter 3: War, Violent Acts, Disease, and Catastrophic Natural Events 85
Chapter 4: Abortion 96
Chapter 5: Dementia and Other Brain Issues 102

PART 4: THE END IS ONLY THE BEGINNING 105

Chapter 1: Who I Really Am 105
Chapter 2: Death as the New Beginning 109
Chapter 3: The Death of Pets 113

EPILOGUE 117
FINAL THOUGHTS 118
REINTERPRETATION OF THE 10 LAWS 119
ABOUT THE AUHTOR 123

DEDICATION

I dedicate this book to all my patients who have passed from this life to the next and to their families who have grieved every single day without them.

I also dedicate this book to all the doctors, nurses, and ancillary healthcare workers who try to stave off their patients' deaths for another day, whether they were successful or not.

Most of all, I dedicate this book to those very brave souls that tend to the dying through hospice care and who make the last few weeks, days, or hours a comfortable transition for their patients as they exit life on this planet. Their work is courageous, for they look Death in the eyes and see the blessing it represents. They're Death's gentle partners.

FOREWARD

"The fear of death is virtually meaningless. We need to have the humility to know that, in death, we're in the company of countless others, and that death is the only certain destiny that awaits us all. I'm not overly preoccupied with death but rather by the enormous question mark it represents. Is it nothingness? That's possible. If it's not, then what a great adventure lies ahead."

—Francois Mitterand, prior to his death from prostate cancer

Here, dear friends, lies the crux of the problem. We fear what we don't know, and we certainly don't know what happens after our physical life ceases. My hope is that by examining this topic through the eyes of Death itself, we may be able to get a better understanding of the *"great adventure [that] lies ahead,"* thereby replacing fear with pure love.

As you read this book, you may wonder how I know what Death is "thinking." I can only describe what some of you might not understand or believe. The words you'll read came from within. I was the scribe, not the author. I interviewed Death, and Death answered my questions.

INTRODUCTION

I've heard it said that we choose our careers based on what we fear most.

I've always feared death, so it makes sense that I chose medicine. In fact, I think I was lying to myself when I thought I wanted to be a doctor to "help people." In retrospect, I now see I also wanted to defeat what I feared most. I thought that by doing that, I'd also be "helping people" in the most powerful way possible.

My daughter, on the other hand, chose nursing. Her fear isn't of death but of the suffering created by illness. Her goal, she once told me, is to be able to hold the hands of her patients, for as long as necessary, in an effort to provide maximum emotional comfort. And therein lies our difference. Although we both want our patients to live, my losing a patient to death seems, to me, a defeat. Her losing her patient, albeit sad, is tempered by her ability to provide comfort and grace in those last days, hours, and moments.

Death has been present in my thoughts from my earliest memories—not always in the forefront, but always there. The interesting part, at least for me, is that throughout most of my life, I've been blessed in that I've only infrequently experienced the death of a close relative or friend. I've been present countless times, however, as my patients transitioned from this life to the next. I've witnessed their last breaths and, in fact, assisted Death by terminating life support in those cases where there was no hope of recovery.

Perhaps it's because of these experiences that I've always been fearful of the prospect of life ending.

I believe that my journey into the study of medicine, therefore, originated with the belief that if I could learn what kept us alive, I could more effectively prevent us from dying—or, at least, prevent an untimely death. To me, each time I defeated Death from taking a patient, I won another battle. I swear there were times after I got a patient through a particular crisis that I could most definitely feel Death brush up against me and whisper in my ear, "Next time... I'll be back next time, and you won't win." There were many times I felt Death's "chill" and wondered when that next time would come. I knew I always needed to be prepared, could never let my guard down, and always had to be vigilant of Death approaching to take another soul so I'd be ready and would win again.

And yet, what evolved as my career progressed has been more of a partnership with Death rather than a constant fight. Yes, I still feel we battle it out at a patient's bedside, and yes, I do feel a sense of victory when I win, but more often than not we've learned to work together. I've learned to accept the relief of suffering that Death brings when the hope for life becomes futile.

In fact, it was a bedside nurse who taught me this. When I was in the midst of one of those "battles," she looked at me and said, "Don't think you're losing. You've done your best, but it's time to let the suffering pass. Your job is to know when Death is your partner, not your enemy." Such wise words, and not dissimilar to what my daughter has expressed to me.

And so, my relationship with Death has evolved from one of constant battle, tallying my victories on a score card, to one of mutual respect for what we each can do for the other and the patient we share. I say this because, as I've come to understand how Death functions, I don't believe It necessarily wants to take lives "just because." On the contrary, I believe Death is actually relieved when I'm able to assist the living to keep living. On some other plane of reality, I believe Death is proud of me when I succeed. I used to think otherwise, but I no longer hear the whispers that It will return. Nor am I fearful that Death will "win." As in any professional relationship, I maintain a certain level of respect for Death. Yet, I also know that despite this mutual respect for each other, I can't let my guard down because Death will always take the opportunity to do what It does best—not with malice but simply because it's Nature's way.

This topic has inspired me to share my experiences with you through my interview with Death to soften your fear of the inevitable. I can't guarantee that this will happen, especially since my own fear hasn't completely dissipated. Even now, when I wake up in the middle of the night, my thoughts turn to the undeniable fact that we're all mortal and that each of us will go through the process of dying alone. I always pray that I won't know that I've died and that I'll pass during sleep so I won't be tortured by regrets and the uncertainty of what's to come.

In the process of having Death relay to me Its thoughts concerning how It is perceived by others and how Death would like to be perceived, It also wanted us to know the historical perspective as well as the latest scientific theories and research on the Soul and it's journey. It's through this science that a better understanding of the concept of the Afterlife may evolve.

I know it seems strange that I'm using Death's perspective of Itself to attempt to dissipate our fear of It. But what better way to understand Death than to ask of It the questions that make us so anxious about what will happen during our final moments. In reality, I believe Death wanted me to do this project. Incredibly, instead of feeling fear as I wrote the words of this book, I felt a certain peace descend over me, a feeling that only a spiritual presence can bestow.

To complete the discussion of Death, we must also bring the religious aspects to light. Asking Death to comment on the understanding of It in the major world religions is important to gain insight into our perceptions and fears. I'm Jewish and, as such, I should have a Jewish perspective in telling these stories. However, Death supersedes all religions. By having Death relay how various religions view It, humanity is represented in its entirety. Biases are eradicated and the truth is revealed.

Finally, asking Death It's views on the controversial topics of suicide, euthanasia, war, disease, and acts of violence may help us better understand these difficult and heartbreaking subjects.

Death will shed further light on human death by presenting examples of documented grief felt by animals—domestic and in the wild—over the death of a member of their community. Because we have the ability to provide our best friends in the animal world with final relief from pain, this should inform our discussions about the practice of euthanasia in humans.

The complex topics of death discussed in this book are all intertwined, just as everything in the living world is intertwined. Most of us have heard of "the butterfly effect," which was introduced in a television commercial in which the flutter of a butterfly's wings was shown affecting actions occurring half a world away. This is, in reality, very true. We'll explore how this concept relates to Death by examining the theory of Biocentrism. This theory helps to explain our relationship with our world, with Death, and with what follows after.

My purpose in writing down Death's own words is to provide you with insider information, as it were, on a topic that's so perplexing—and often taboo—and yet is an integral part of all life, from the most basic organism to the most complex—human beings. By asking Death pointed questions and allowing Death to answer through these stories, you'll hear, first hand, Death's sage advice to you, the reader. In other words, the answers were not directed to me, but to you. You may believe, or not, that Death spoke directly to me. I only hope the following questions and answers bring new ideas to the table and allow for a gentler and more peaceful relationship with Death.

I also want to clarify that I have used, throughout this book, more religious generic names for the Almighty, first of all so as not to offend any one group, but more importantly, these are the names used by Death. You can interject whatever name is most comfortable for you to understand the concepts presented. Please understand, the names are not what are important, the concepts, however, are.

From this point forward, I'll ask questions and Death will respond in the first person as I, Me, or Myself.

I now turn this book over to Death.

PART 1: MEDICAL TRAINING AND BEYOND

Question: Could You please tell the reader what You want us to take away from the stories we're about to hear?

Answer:

Do I, Death, inspire the collective "you" to love life, or do I have the opposite effect and scare you into attempting to believe you're immortal? This is the question you must first ask yourselves when you talk about Me.

If you fear Me, you can't enjoy your life's journey because the destination is unacceptable.

If you embrace that your destination allows you to experience a fantastic journey called your life, then that journey will be one of joy and learning.

The stories I'll relate to you in these subsequent chapters, which were experienced by My scribe, CC, a physician, have helped Me to understand how you perceive Me and why you fear Me.

My hope is that as I tell these stories from My perspective, you can begin to better understand the relationship between rejoicing in your life and fearing Me.

Because truly, in the end, life is too short to live in constant fear.

These stories center around CC from her early days as a medical student through the present day. She's been a well-established physician of over 30 years. She's allowed Me to speak through her to the degree that she, as a human, is able to articulate My thoughts.

I address CC in the third person when answering her questions because the answers are meant for everyone, not just CC. It is through CC's experiences and her questions of Me, that I can explain Myself to the world, as I, Death want to be viewed.

Chapter 1: Medical School—The Early Experiences

Question: How did the visceral experience that CC and her colleagues had upon seeing a dead person for the first time affect how You were perceived and accepted by them?

Answer:

I wish I could tell you that I gently introduced Myself to the gaggle of medical students as they first started on their journey in the healing sciences. Alas, that wasn't the case. Granted, the experiences I'm relaying occurred at an offshore medical school that CC and her classmates attended. In fact, I believe it was because they were at this school that they were particularly traumatized unlike their compatriots who attended American schools.

For that, I'm sorry, but there's never an easy way to introduce Myself. Had they discussed their experiences with other medical students, they probably would have found those students experienced equally traumatizing stories played out in different circumstances. Although many years have passed since these first horrific memories, members of that class often revisit this first encounter with Me. I guess, in actuality, it was more a nightmare than a memory, even by My standards, and so it's an important story to tell.

Let Me recount for you that initial traumatizing experience. Imagine being a first-year medical student, imbued with all the altruistic qualities associated with this pursuit. These kids were fresh, ready to learn, hoping that their post-graduate education would teach them how they could better help others. Now, imagine a group of these same students, walking past a trap door in the hallway floor between classrooms that connected to a basement. Most times, this door was closed. One day, however, they happened to walk by when the trap door was open. A worker had just descended the stairs into the basement. What they saw shocked them so badly they stood there transfixed, staring down into the room below.

Workers were throwing the bodies of babies around to each other in a sort of processing line, where they were sorted by size. The bodies were being washed with hoses and scrubbed with rough bristle brushes. These weren't mannequins. They were the bodies of dead babies, unceremoniously being prepared for autopsy.

I was unhappy that these sensitive, naïve students had to see this. I was especially unhappy that I was being disrespected in such a way. How dare they show such callousness toward My work! Even though the Souls of these little ones were already with Me, the bodies still deserved respect.

And so, in this unfortunate way, the training of these students began. The callousness they observed that day taught them their first lesson. And what was that lesson? The absolute necessity for reverence when in My company, which clearly isn't happening if dead bodies are being thrown around. That day, I heard the Souls of these students vow to never view Me other than with the utmost respect—both in their perception of the person who had just died and of the family of that person. Since this lesson had to be learned, what better why to teach it than by using shock value?

Those students wondered, at the time, where the families of those babies were. I knew these departed Souls were the products of term pregnancies—babies that had died soon after birth. Unfortunately, they'd been born into poor families that couldn't afford a funeral or families that believed they were assisting scientific discovery. They were, but not in the way they or I assumed.

That day, those babies taught these new students to feel compassion and respect in My presence, along with reverence for life. And although they went on to learn anatomy with bodies that were assigned to them for the purpose of performing autopsies, they never forgot to be thankful to the dead, because each time they used the bodies given to them for this task, they knew they were continuing to learn the lessons that would someday help the living.

You might wonder, "Why, if the Soul has already been taken by Me, would it matter what happens to the body?" Certainly, your cultures since the beginning of conscious thought, have had rituals surrounding the preparation and burials of those who have died. The respect shown to a body is simply an extension of the respect given to the Soul that has come with Me. Therefore, the idea, which is quite accurate, is that by disrespecting the body, you are in essence, disrespecting the Soul.
You may not realize that your memorials and customs are actually not only comforting to those left behind, but to the Souls themselves.

Question: How did seeing a culture treat death as a normal part of life rather than as a tragedy continue to mold the perception of who You were and continue to be for these students?

Answer:

Well, interestingly, later on during that first semester when I was visiting a small, rural town, these same students arrived to start practicing their new skills by taking patient histories and performing physical examinations. The work of these students was considered "social service," because this rural population had never seen medical personnel. Understand that in this Third World country, rural areas consisted of homes where there was no running water and no electricity. These "homes" only had three walls, dirt floors, and thatched or tin roofs. The nearby creek that was used to wash clothes and dishes was also the communal bathtub. The water was filthy and full of parasites, and so a significant portion of the population was infected with these same parasites. These organisms would, in the final stages of infection, invade the liver and brain. Death wasn't an uncommon consequence, thus My visit.

And so it was that on one morning, on the way to the local school to examine children and teach them the importance of hygiene, these medical students witnessed a family procession walking with a small, white coffin that obviously held the body of a child. There were no tears. On the contrary, it almost appeared to be a casual walk through the town to the grave site. As these students watched, they understood that, in this village, I, Death, was just another part of everyday life, an expected visitor and not a cause for emotional outbursts. This acceptance of death shocked them as much as their previous encounter with Me at their school.

I read their minds and saw they were asking themselves, "What's this scene supposed to teach us? Is it teaching us that Death should be seen as a natural process and therefore to be treated casually?" How could they accept this view when their ultimate goal in going to medical school was to prevent Me from visiting their patients prematurely?

The students left this town a couple of weeks later, quite perplexed by all they'd witnessed. Nonetheless, I believe that both these early experiences allowed them to begin to form serious impressions of what I represented, which was different for each of them. They were asking themselves how these experiences affected them, personally and professionally. The answer lay within each of them and was revealed as they continued on their journey toward becoming physicians.

Question: How did the unnecessary pain and suffering of animals used for teaching these students change the perception they had about the job You do?

Answer:

When humans talk about the end of life, most include their feelings about animal best friends—the dogs, cats, and other sundry pets in their lives. I want to add this story because it highlights the fact that animals play a significant role in how humans process what happens when a living thing begins the dying process, how they can assist to end suffering, and why you wish to believe that the end of life is not the ultimate end. In other words, you, as humans, want to know that your relationships with those you love—whether human or animal—will continue in some form after the physical body is gone. I'll discuss this now and then in more in depth in a later chapter.

This story exemplifies the depth of feeling for all living things that humans can achieve, especially when they're in training to become healers. It also demonstrates how they're beginning to view Me—not always as a badass taking life away but instead more like a savior that relieves pain and suffering. Clearly, this is an important lesson to learn.

These same students were in their third year of medical school, and the labs they were engaged in at that time centered on surgical procedures. There were no virtual models to practice on in those days. Students were given dogs obtained from the pound on which to practice surgical techniques. I could tell that their first go-around was difficult for them, at best, even though the animals were well sedated.

This practice was especially difficult for CC, who had a bleeding heart for all animals. As the labs continued through the week and the same animals were used for different surgical procedures until they were finally euthanized to end their misery, it became increasingly difficult for the students to perform their tasks—let alone learn—because of the empathy they felt. By the end of the week, CC had decided to lead the group in boycotting the lab course and refusing to do any further surgical procedures on any new animals they were given, even if that meant they might fail the class. They put up such a stink that they were granted their wish to no longer use live specimens. For the rest of that semester, they practiced their surgical techniques on dead animals and human corpses used for anatomy classes. They felt gratified that they were no longer causing unnecessary pain and suffering for innocent living things.

Why did this matter to them so much? After all, these dogs weren't their pets and they had no emotional ties to them. Yet they cared enough to possibly flunk a class to protect innocent lives from suffering.

I believe that through this particular experience, these students realized I wasn't so bad after all! They realized that living things experiencing pain and suffering engender a great deal of empathy on those who are part of such experiences, especially when innocent animals are involved. It also highlighted that these students preferred to see Me take over and bring peace to the suffering animal rather than have it continue. That was a pretty powerful lesson and one where, for the first time, I wasn't seen as the villain but rather as the savior. Even though these students may not have fully realized this at the time, I can assure you they do now.

Question: What was the impact You had on these young students, seeing Your work first-hand?

Answer:

Let Me tell you, I packed a wallop! The following story took place during the clerkship period in which CC and her group were involved before their residencies started.

CC was working with another medical student as "scuts," which is what the residents used to call medical students who shadowed them during clerkships. They were doing a night shift and were asked to do a blood gas evaluation on an elderly patient. She'd been admitted for pneumonia from a nearby nursing home. She didn't have a living will, because these types of directives didn't exist back then. All patients were routinely resuscitated. It was a rare case in which you'd hear of the family having a "do not resuscitate" directive in place for an elderly relative.

CC's partner went to do the blood gas test while CC went on an errand for the resident. A few minutes later, this other student paged CC and told her she couldn't get the blood gas done and could she please come help so this chore would be over and she could move on to the next procedure she'd been asked to do. This particular patient was in a double room with another elderly patient. I watched with great interest, because the elderly woman with pneumonia was already in My company.

When CC arrived, she realized immediately that this patient was in extremis, which means she was breathing her last breaths. These "breaths" were actually spinal reflexes, which meant the patient was already dead and with Me.

In CC's naivety, she said rather loudly to the other medical student, "She's already dead! You can't get a blood gas because she has no pulse!" Unfortunately, her lack of discretion in yelling this to the other student scared the other patient in the room, who jumped out of bed and went screaming out the door. Of course, CC was ever so embarrassed and sorry that she'd exhibited such a paucity of compassion in not considering the feelings of this patient's roommate. I wish I could have made all involved feel better by conveying to them that this patient was finally at peace. But, alas, I couldn't reach out to them and was relegated to watch the distress of all involved—students and the terrified roommate.

At the time, I wondered why CC reacted so poorly despite the previous experiences she'd had, as I described above. I believe she was still acting from her fear of who I was and what I did. She also didn't yet know how to deal with coming face to face not with a dead person but with a person who was in her final moments of life and about to die—a person who, a few minutes before, was still very much alive. I think she knew I was around, watching, and that frightened her too. I also believe the fear generated in this chance encounter with Me stemmed from the fact the elderly person had died alone, with no loved ones holding her hand, easing her into the other world. CC didn't realize that I comfort all My citizens of the Afterlife. She was frightened by the prospect of a patient dying alone more than the finality that I bring.

I think this was a pivotal case for CC, one that she thinks of often when she encounters Me in the patients she's taking care of. These days, her patients are newborns, which means CC has the ability to hold them in her arms or ask that one of the nurses hold them as I take the little one from its short life. They do this if their families are too frightened to hold them or their religion doesn't allow them to hold a dying person. The saddest cases are when the babies have no family members around to comfort them at the end. The lesson learned with these little ones has allowed CC to eventually become less scared of Me. She now respectfully allows Me to do My job while she or others provide comfort on this side of the veil, knowing I'll provide comfort forever on the other side.

Question: How did these students react when they realized that professionals who were supposed to help deter Your work inadvertently assisted You?

Answer:

I remember an exceptionally difficult experience that CC and her classmates had while on a surgical rotation. This particular case was made even more traumatic because CC and her classmates had connected personally with this patient prior to her going into surgery to remove a part of her lung affected by both a tumor and an abscess. This patient was a heavy smoker, and the first step in her treatment prior to starting any chemo or radiation therapy was removal of the large tumor and draining the abscess.

The patient was a religious person and was holding her rosary beads and praying she'd make it out of surgery. I was watching this scene at a distance, knowing she'd be with Me soon. I watched CC hold this patient's hand and comfort her, telling her that of course she'd make it through the surgery. CC told her she'd do great and they'd talk afterward. She could tell this patient was frightened and didn't want her life to be over so soon. She had so much more she wanted to do, and she had things she wanted to say to her loved ones. She sensed she might not have the opportunity to do so.

This is the part of My job that's so difficult. Among the best advice I've heard humans give is that everyone should live their lives as if each moment is their last. Live so you don't have any regrets if your life were to end at this moment. I'm not able to postpone your departure just because you haven't said your proper goodbyes or made peace with others. I'll take you with me as has been planned by the Higher Source of the Universe.

Anyway, CC and another classmate watched as the anesthesiologist placed the breathing tube in this patient's throat and put her under. The students and I remember the anesthesiologist telling the surgeon he could begin. It wasn't long before everything went wrong. Once inside the patient's lung, the surgeon found the tumor and abscess. However, because of his inexperience, the anesthesiologist was totally unprepared for what happened next. Instead of protecting the patient's good lung by placing the breathing tube into the airway entering the unaffected lung, he left the breathing tube in the main airway called the bronchus. As the surgeon began to remove the abscess, the worst happened. The abscess ruptured into the bronchus and starting draining into the good lung that had been unaffected by disease. At that point, the anesthesiologist lost total control of the patency of the patient's airway—so much so that he was unable to successfully suction the pus pouring out. In effect, his patient was drowning and he was powerless to reverse the process. The patient's oxygen levels dropped and her heart rate started failing. Not long after this catastrophic event started, the patient died on the table.

CC, her classmates, and the family never had the opportunity to talk to her again, nor did this patient have the opportunity to speak to her family. We all watched as the surgeon came out of the operating room to tell the family their loved one had died. They all saw their devastated faces. I wish I could have eased everyone's mind and tell them it was inevitable and moreover, that she would have passed eventually and in a great deal of pain had she survived the surgery. I wish I could have given them peace of mind that their family member had died peacefully and she was now free of worry and pain. But there was much left unsaid between this patient and her family, and that's what made this a tragedy.

It was sad for Me, too. I was sad that CC and her classmates had to learn the hard way that because of the inexperience of one person, a patient died unnecessarily. This case is ever present in these now "seasoned" doctor's minds when making decisions during rounds or emergency situations. The possibility that any one of them could unwittingly help Me to take one of their patients has kept them vigilant to the fact that they must always be at their best and never assume they know everything. In evaluating a situation, they now run through a multitude of scenarios in their minds that might adversely affect the outcome of their patient. They could never accept or forgive themselves if a patient died because of their carelessness, lack of knowledge, or ineptitude. Unfortunately, they still are witnesses to the consequences of ignorance, arrogance, or both—and I'm usually on the scene when that happens.

To this day, when CC teaches residents, she always tells them, "If you learn only one thing from me, I want it to be this: Be aware of the profound impact our decisions have on others. We're not baking cookies so that if you burn a batch you can bake new ones. In caring for a patient, everything you do or think of doing affects the outcome of that patient for the rest of their lives. It may even cause an untimely death. You can't re-create that life nor can you start over. The decisions you make are critical and, most of the time, they can't be reversed."

Interestingly, the other piece of wisdom she wants her students to always remember is, "There are worse things than dying."

With her first "pearl of wisdom," it's obvious that CC wants her students to understand the enormity of their decisions and the importance of not allowing arrogance, ego, laziness, or ignorance to govern their thinking. She also wants them to understand that what they do is vitally important and should never be considered "just a job." Behind every disease they treat is a patient who wants to be well and has loved ones that are depending on the doctor to make this happen. She wants them to learn that it's not the final outcome—death—they should fear. It's that this outcome is unacceptable when it results from human carelessness. Such an outcome is the ultimate insult to life.

Her second pearl of wisdom is just as important because CC is helping her students to not fear Me as she feared Me for a significant portion of her career. She tries to teach her students not to consider Me as their enemy but as their partner—a realization that's taken her a long time to figure out.

And so, because of these early experiences, CC and her fellow students learned to respect Me. She and her colleagues came to understand that through the decisions they made for each patient, they either assisted Me or were able to keep Me at bay for a bit longer. However, despite gaining respect for Me, they still feared Me. It wasn't until later in their careers that they began to see Me as their partner. As they became more introspective about their experiences with me and what these experiences meant to them, their attitudes changed. Even now, as I narrate these words, I realize that during the time of their training they were gaining insight into what these experiences were teaching them about Me, eventually allowing them to accept Me, not as an enemy, but as a colleague.

However, during the time they were still learning, they continued to consider Me, for the most part, as their enemy. Thankfully, fear was no longer the dominant feeling when they confronted Me, but they hadn't yet embraced the entire scope of the being I was, am and will always be. So, let's continue, and you'll see how they came to know Me better.

Chapter 2: Residency and Fellowship—Continuing Early Experiences

Question: What other stories can You tell us that demonstrate how the experiences of these young physicians continued to shape how they perceived You?

Answer:

Residency. Wow. This was the first time these young people were called "doctor" and it meant something. They were all still wet behind the ears and barely able to keep themselves alive, let alone save others. They learned so much back then. This is when the type of physician they'd eventually become—caring or indifferent, humble or arrogant—was revealed. I know this because I was around them constantly, watching and waiting.

There were two centers of excellence within CC's pediatric hospital; one was the Cystic Fibrosis Center and the other was the Hematology/Oncology Center for childhood cancers. Life-and-death dramas occurred frequently in both these places, and she witnessed many of them—and at times was intimately involved.

As a side note, her fellowship training seemed much tamer than her residency training, and her memories of that experience were much fuzzier, as if she'd had to readjust the lens of her camera and could never get it quite right. In actuality, what happened was that in residency, she was mostly flying by the seat of her pants. She had little supervision and many times was left to figure out things for herself, with—if she was lucky—a little help from the senior residents. In her fellowship (which involved sub-specialty training), she was heavily supervised and had little decision-making responsibility. What the attending physician dictated was done. During that time, CC's learning came from books more than from patients. Life-and-death decisions had been less frequent than she experienced as a resident. It wasn't until she became an "attending" herself that the power of her learning escalated exponentially—both in lessons about preserving life as well as lessons about Me, My role, and the evolution of our relationship.

Question: How did You teach CC and others that Grace is an integral part of who You are?

Answer:

I can answer that in three words: The cancer ward. One of CC's first encounters with pediatric cancer involved a little girl who was about four years old. She had a history of chronic ear infections that were treated with a common antibiotic. This antibiotic was known to have an adverse effect if used too often. It suppressed the bone marrow from producing blood cells, and patients routinely became anemic (low red cells) as well as neutropenic (low white cells) and thrombocytopenic (low platelets). Because of this, doctors now rarely use this antibiotic, as there are other, newer classes of antibiotics better suited to address the diverse cornucopia of bacteria we see today. However, back then, it was their best line of defense against chronic otitis media (ear infections).

Although the antibiotic had the beneficial effect of stopping subsequent ear infections in this little girl (infections which had become dangerously close to causing meningitis because of the invasion of the bacteria into her sinuses), it also produced the adverse effects described above. Her bone marrow became permanently suppressed and she stopped producing any red or white blood cells. CC and her team began her treatment by giving her transfusions a few times a month, but, eventually, these transfusions became more frequent until they were required daily. By that time, within a few hours of transfusion, her body was again devoid of these vital blood cells, destroyed by her own body as foreign. As you know, without red cells, the blood can't carry oxygen from the lungs to the rest of the body and, without white cells and platelets, it can't protect the body from infections nor does blood clot properly. The smallest cut can become a crisis.

As the little girl's transfusions became more frequent, she became sicker—she developed pancytopenia (devoid of all blood cells). That's when My watch began. They had to do bone marrow tests to see if the chemotherapy treatments she was receiving were helping her bone marrow to recover. It never did.

Late one night, when CC was on call, this little girl's IV, which allowed her to receive the blood transfusions she needed to survive, became dislodged. CC worked desperately to re-insert the child's life-giving intravenous line, with no success. She finally made a call to her hematology/oncology attending to see what other options they had. He simply stated to her on the phone, "This situation is life or death for this little girl. If you're unable to replace her IV, she won't make it though the night."

CC returned to this little girl's room and explained to the child that she had to try again to get the IV started. Throughout this ordeal, the little girl had been crying because each attempt had been so painful. However, this time, the child looked at CC calmly and, as only an old soul in a four-year-old body could do, said, "OK, I trust you. I know you can put this IV in. I know I need it. I'll be good and stay still."

Before attempting to insert the needle, I heard CC say a prayer to a Higher Source to help guide her hand. She didn't want the child to die on her watch. She'd have forever felt responsible for ending her life. That night, she was guided by that Higher Source, and the IV slipped easily into a vein, even though CC could barely see beneath the skin of the girl's swollen hand. Her life-saving transfusion was started, and I stood watch as they both slept that night with the knowledge I wasn't going to take that child with me just yet.

Of course, they didn't know I continued keeping watch. Most don't realize that My job isn't only to take a person away when their time has come but also to calm them and help ease the transition to their final journey, when the time is near to take the final journey with Me. So, that night, I calmed the little girl with thoughts that she was loved.

The next morning, all the residents who'd taken care of this young patient knew her time was nearing the end, and I watched as they gathered in her room to say their goodbyes. She was so thankful to all of them for their jokes, for trying to keep her smiling and laughing despite the worst of the worst that any child and parent would ever face. As she took her last breath, they placed a single red rose and her favorite stuffed toy in her hand and said farewell to a very brave little girl. At that moment, I took her from her pain and brought her into the loving arms of The Universal Source of Love, Peace, and Light.

I know CC and the other residents who'd helped take care of this girl were very angry at Me for taking away such a young life. But it wasn't My fault. The dye had been cast long ago when this little girl battled one ear infection after another. To CC, however, her death seemed so unnecessary. She didn't understand what benefit there could be in this little girl's death. She felt betrayed that her medical knowledge could do nothing to save her. And so each experience with a dying patient continued to heighten her personal battle with Me.

What she didn't realize at that time was that, through this little girl, I taught CC the meaning of dignity in death. The Grace involved in her passing was My lesson to all of them. To live life to the fullest, it must be appreciated every second of every day. This little girl didn't die crying, pleading that she wanted to live longer or that she was afraid to die. Instead, her last words to those around her were of gratitude for making her moments in the hospital as happy as possible. When she passed, she actually had a smile on her face. She was happy to be with Me. Her battles were finally over, as were her pain and suffering.

At that time, however, the doctors who'd cared for her couldn't understand this perspective. They, as residents, were angry at their "failure." It would take many more experiences with Me before CC and her colleagues would come to the realization that the lessons taught by Me would allow them to eventually make peace with My role not as the villain but rather the "superhero", taking Souls away from the physical pain of their life on earth and bringing peace and comfort instead.

Question: Can You explain the following description of Yourself? "I offer no apologies; I offer no explanations. I am what I am."

Answer:

Certainly. Perhaps the following story will help illustrate who I really am.

When CC was in the cancer ward, I'm was, of course, with her more than she could imagine. I wish she would have trusted me to help her with her more difficult patients. One of these was a little boy, just five years old, recently admitted with leukemia. He was adorable, and his parents couldn't have been more supportive and accepting of his diagnosis despite the poor rates of survival for children with this disease in the early 1980s. The little boy's father was a minister and felt that the Lord would provide his son and the family with all the comfort and strength needed to move onward to fight and win this battle.

The chemo treatment began and, initially, everything was going well. In fact, soon into his therapy, the child's doctors managed to suppress the bone marrow and cause a temporary reprieve from the continuous proliferation of the leukemic cells.

Unfortunately, as the boy's white cells diminished, his risk of infection increased drastically and he developed a severe complication called necrotizing fasciitis. This means that the layers of tissue under the skin became infected and began to slough off, as did his skin. This condition is painful and spreads quickly to large areas of the body. His started in the groin area and continued up the abdomen to the chest.

CC's team was losing the battle quickly and completely, not because the leukemia was uncontrolled but because their expert removal of his white cells with the chemo had caused him to have this massive, uncontrollable infection. You see, if there are no white cells, antibiotics are rendered almost ineffective to work against bacteria. It's a fine balance that must be maintained between a human's own cells and the medicine to affect the response needed.

The child was dying and his parents knew it. Despite this, the dad continued to pray and praise the Lord for His gifts.

That night, the boy's mom decided to stay at the hospital to keep her son company. The dad needed to prepare his sermon, since the next day was Sunday, so he wasn't present. CC spoke to the mom and explained they'd continue to do everything in their power to treat the infection so her son could remain in remission and, hopefully, win his battle against leukemia. The mother

thanked CC and said, "You know, I think I need to lie down for a while because I have a bad headache right now. I think the stress of everything has finally caught up with me. Hopefully, some sleep will help me feel more refreshed." CC found her an empty patient room on the ward close to her son and promised her she'd wake her up if anything changed in her son's condition.
I kept this mom company that night. She never did wake up. A nurse found her the next morning in the bed CC had found for her the previous night to sleep. She had, in fact, died in her sleep. Her autopsy showed severe viral meningitis with subsequent brain herniation.

I watched as the hematology/oncology team broke the news to the father, and, instead of getting angry, the dad praised God for all His kindness and love. His son died soon after. I had, in essence, taken his family from him in the span of one week, yet the man expressed no anger. Instead, he thanked the team for all their efforts. He knew that both his son and wife were in a better place. He didn't feel as CC and the others in the medical team did, that I'd been selfish and greedy.

I was sad to see that, again, anger was the only emotion CC felt at this turn of events. All she could think about was how many bad things seemed to be happening to this one family and how impossible it was to feel anything but anger at her powerlessness in the situation. And yet, this father didn't feel this way, nor did his extended family that came to help him with the arrangements that needed to be made. This wasn't lost on CC or the others. They thought about what this could all mean and what lessons they could take away with them.

So what did this experience teach CC and the others in the healthcare team? Back then, she and the others weren't sure. Later on, as they looked back on this horrendous experience, they came to be at peace with the fact that, as humans, we simply don't know the "why" of everything. So, do you the reader, believe that's a good enough answer? Allow Me to answer this for you. Essentially, this experience ended up teaching CC and the others that although humans don't know what really comes after I visit (we'll delve into this in the second part of the book), theirs isn't to reason the how or why but instead to simply have faith in life itself, as short as it might be, and the preciousness of every minute lived. Perhaps if CC and the others had the maturity then to sit down with this pastor father and ask him where his faith came from, he might have educated them as to how we humans are meant to celebrate life always and in all circumstances.

Let Me reiterate the importance of this concept.
To have the ability to be thankful for waking up in the morning, living another day, and making a difference in the world; to be allowed to kiss loved ones and tell them how much they're loved—these are the blessings that humans should focus on. They shouldn't focus on the

fact that I appeared and unfairly took someone too early from them, or that their loved one was prevented from living another day, week, month, or year. Humans have difficulty grasping this concept, even as they get older and supposedly wiser. I'd venture to say that some, even on their death beds, will never understand this concept and will die a miserable death believing they've been cheated of more time being alive. In reality, life was given to them for many years, and it was they who chose not to live it fully.

What might you, the reader, learn from this experience? Do you feel I've given an adequate explanation of who I am and what I do? Think about this story again and then examine your life and how you live it. Do you live each day to the fullest? Or do you live waiting for the next moment to make you happy, or that this or that material thing or accomplishment will make you happy once you get it? Live life now, enjoy each moment now, and make each day important to you and the people around you. Make a lasting difference in someone's life, in your community, in your world. Always remember, life is to be enjoyed for it's journey, not it's destination, because, dear ones, I am that destination.

As you know, I'm a harsh teacher. Not many chances are given to you to learn what I have to teach. When you're hit with this revelation of the preciousness of life, take it and run with it. You might even outrun Me, at least for a little while. I'll eventually catch up to you, but, when I do, you'll go with Me to a new existence, happy in the knowledge that you made every day count in the here and now. Remember, I am what I am, and I make no excuses. Nor should you.

Question: Do You do Your job by Yourself, or do You require others, such as a human "community," to help Your job go smoothly?

Answer:

What an interesting and thoughtful question!

Let Me try to explain with another story.

Back in the day when CC was a resident, cystic fibrosis (CF) was as dire a diagnosis as cancer. It was close to impossible for a CF patient to make it beyond adolescence and none made it to adulthood. The promise of a bright future, getting married, and starting a family was dashed if a child was diagnosed with CF. Parents knew this, and they either spoiled the child, knowing its life would be short, or there was an element of subconscious non-bonding that occurred because the prospect of the loss was too great to bear. After all, how could you explain to a child that they'd never go to college, experience sex, fall in love, get married, have a job, or have children? Even if you could, would you tell them this or would you lie to them? Despite what adults might think about the innocence of children, they sense and demand the truth. They may feign ignorance so as not to worry their parents, but they know.

Such was the case with a young CF patient under CC's care when she was a resident. He'd miraculously made it into his early teens and he no longer wanted to be treated like a child. He wanted to have a better understanding of his illness and what it would ultimately mean for him. However, it was difficult to have conversations with him, not only because he tired quickly between his fits of coughing when he tried to talk but because it was so emotionally taxing to discuss with him end-of-life issues. You see, his parents couldn't deal with his illness well and, although they visited, these visits were brief. Eventually his parents divorced because of his illness, and the guilt he felt for this turn of events was significant.

During this young man's last stay with CC and her team, they had to place tubes through his chest wall because his lungs were collapsing from the scar tissue that had formed over years of mucous building up and blocking his airways. Soon after this, the young man died. For CC and the other caretakers, his death was sad not only because his life and the promise of a bright future had been cut short but because he died feeling sad for himself. He knew he'd not had the opportunity to live any real life at all.

Certainly, he taught CC that life is precious and must be appreciated at all times. But even more, this young man taught CC that every patient deserves a supportive community, particularly when life is ending. A community becomes that much more important when it's time to help individuals transition to the other side. He taught CC that leaving this world can be very lonely and sad if it seems no one cares about you, even if, in actuality, they do care but are too fearful to show it.

And that brings Me to the next point. My greatest wish is for humans to not fear those who are dying. The dying need support more than ever during those final days up to and after I come to take them. Many people fear the dying and don't want to face them. Sharing those last precious few days and moments of the person leaving helps immortalize them in the memory of their loved ones. This is so very important. My greatest wish is that I'm no longer feared and looked upon as the Grim Reaper, taking life unjustly and leaving nothing but grief for those who remain. I understand that when humans have this vision of Me, they avoid the dying person because they fear Me. Mortality smacks them square in the face when they face someone who is dying and mortality equals finality. You are wrong. Mortality only equals finality of this life, not the life I will bring you to. Instead, I hope that by understanding that I'm Light, Love, and Grace and am present to bring the dying person to a better place, the living can help Me comfort the dying and give them peace, knowing their Soul will continue on.

Question: Is there any way that Your job can be made more acceptable? Would it help if the community rallies around those left behind?

Answer:

As I've said before, I frighten humans. They don't like to talk about Me or what My job ultimately means. Those with little or no first-hand experience of My presence are fearful that I might be as contagious as the Black Plague. But how do you explain the fear of those who live in My presence daily? Perhaps those who can make a difference in nurturing life actually feel My power even more because I make them aware of their powerlessness.

I remember following CC when she was a resident working in the Neonatal Intensive Care Nursery (NICU). I remember her running to assist with the delivery of a premature infant of 28 weeks gestation. In the 80s, this extreme prematurity meant close to 100% mortality. These days, such babies have close to the same survival rates as a full-term infant. Anyway, I remember her running into the NICU with this baby into which she'd placed a breathing tube immediately after delivery, only to have the NICU nurse look at her with disgust and say, "What are you bringing me this fetus for? He'll die anyway. Why are we wasting our time with this?"

In fact, I did take the baby away. You can't save a life in such a difficult situation if some of the members of your team aren't motivated to do so. Those are the times I need to take over. Believe me, I don't consider those times a victory. I'm often a reluctant servant of the Higher Source. However, My primary role is to bring that Soul to the Higher Source and into the healing Light that removes all pain and suffering.

In a similar situation, I remember CC being called to a community hospital to attend to a baby born with a congenital heart defect. She found the baby, who was blue, in a room by itself with little monitoring. Standing nearby was a nurse who was frightened to death of a dying baby (no pun intended)! Thankfully, that baby survived. Again, fear can eliminate the chances of survival and force Me to act, prematurely, as was almost the case in this situation.

I remember taking another baby right out of CC's hands, literally, while she was attempting to exchange his blood to remove the bacterial toxins that were rendering his lungs useless. Was she ever mad at Me! Had I materialized, I'm not sure I'd have survived her attack. However, I knew that little one wouldn't overcome the ravages of the infection. Those toxins had already destroyed the baby's brain, and its body was simply a vehicle for the bacterial growth. I took that one swiftly, because to do otherwise would have been a travesty for both CC and the baby.

I also remember taking a baby with Me that was delivered early because his mother, who'd been diagnosed with metastatic cancer, was administered a chemotherapy drug into her spinal fluid that was meant to be administered into her bloodstream. When the drug reached her brain, the brain was instantly liquefied. Her body was kept alive via mechanical support until the baby reached an age of gestation where it seemed possible for CC to save him. He didn't survive, and both he and his mom were buried in the same coffin.

None of these are My proudest moments. I wish I'd not had to intervene in any of these cases. A life should never be wasted. Please understand that My role is one of easing pain and ending misery when there's no chance to reverse the outcome. I need to emphasize that I don't make the decision who to take. I'm only sent as needed. The ultimate decision is made by the Higher Source, The Universe, the Eternal Light. I'll discuss this more in a later chapter.

Going back to the NICU, there were many more examples I could tell you about. After all, neonates in peril were and continue to be CC's passion and expertise. I continue to follow her around just as I follow all the doctors, nurses, and caretakers at facilities throughout the world that strive to save the lives of people of all ages.

What's been interesting to Me in CC's cases, especially in the early days of her career, was that the beginning of life was seen by many not as an opportunity to clearly make an impressive difference (after all, if babies survive, they have the opportunity for a full life) but instead was seen as creating suffering in an innocent being, a being that couldn't understand why the suffering and pain was occurring. So, the emphasis, years ago when neonatology was still a new specialty, wasn't really on prolonging life but rather on assisting Me to take these little ones so they wouldn't suffer anymore. Let Me be clear: I do not, nor will I ever, need assistance with My job, even when I'm overwhelmed. I get My job done as swiftly and efficiently as possible all by Myself.

What did these experiences in neonatal losses teach CC? These experiences have collectively taught and continue to teach her not to take even the shortest of lives for granted. All humans are equally deserving of help in fighting for life when, and let Me emphasize the word when, there is hope for survival. And it is these patients that require doctors to be their advocates.

Many people have asked CC why she does what she does and how she's able to continue to do it, given that her patients are in such precarious condition. "Isn't it sad to deal with the death of a baby?" they ask. Her response has always been that she feels privileged to participate in thwarting My involvement as often and as much as possible. But the caveat for her is that if I do take one of her patients, the knowledge that she tried to assist life is reward enough. The outcome is what is meant to be, for whatever reason the Universe chooses to make that decision. She also feels that these young patients have created few, if any, memories for themselves or their families. This, she believes, is in contrast to older children and adults. In these older cases, when a patient loses the battle for life, parents, families, and friends are left with many memories of wonderful years lived together, and this can be exceedingly painful. To CC, this is so much harder and sadder than the former situation. It is for Me, too. This is when I need the living to understand their role as comforters of the bereaved. Without this help from humans, My job is intensely more difficult and distasteful.

Question: Please describe a personal example of when Your presence is unnecessary and avoidable.

Answer:

I've already given you a few examples. However, let Me tell you another story that might highlight when My role is warranted and when My role is tragically and prematurely forced upon a human by others not doing their best.

Physicians have always learned to methodically deal with an emergency situation requiring resuscitation by following a protocol known as ABC: Airway, Breathing, and Circulation. When they deviate from this, trouble ensues.

In CC's third year of pediatric residency, when she was a senior resident and close to becoming an attending, she was sent to a community hospital where a six-year-old was undergoing resuscitation, without success. Of course, I was standing by, waiting to take him and end his suffering. Needless to say CC, was scared sh-tless, fretting about what she was going to encounter when she arrived at this hospital's ER.

Nothing had prepared her for what she experienced. When her team arrived, they found this little boy's chest sliced open, his ribs cracked, and his heart being pumped by hand to maintain circulation. At the same time, he had a tube in his throat, presumably in his airway, to maintain an adequate oxygen level. However, the child was blue, and as CC watched them bag in 100% oxygen, she noticed his lungs didn't appear to inflate.

Trying to regain her composure, she asked if anyone had gotten an x-ray to confirm appropriate placement of the breathing tube. The answer shocked her. No, that hadn't been done. The B (breathing) had been addressed as had the C (circulation), but the basic first step, A (airway), was simply assumed to be correct. An x-ray was taken and confirmed what CC had feared: the tube was in fact in the child's stomach.

She pulled out the tube and inserted it into the main airway. Instantly the child became pink. The chest was closed with a manual covering and she ran out of there with the child, heading for her trauma center. I accompanied them the whole way because, in actuality, this little boy had been placed in My charge just before CC arrived. His brain had been deprived of oxygen for too long and had ceased functioning. He needed to come with Me to a better place, because his body no longer served him.

After I took him, CC kept asking, "Why did this happen?" Was it the fear of a boy dying in their care that caused the team at the hospital to forget the basic protocol for resuscitation? What did this teach her? It taught her that I shouldn't have been there, that the outcome was preventable. What did My presence mean in this situation?

Perhaps the explanation is as simple as human fear. When fear takes over thinking, faulty decisions occur. Stated differently, the fear of My presence can cause paralysis in the thoughts and actions of those attempting to deliver care and can inadvertently cause poor decisions that have fatal outcomes. I can't change mistakes made by people. I'm there to clean up the mess and make it right for the Universe. Life is fragile. It can break into pieces if not tended to correctly, and I'm the ultimate janitor, so to speak. Please understand that I'm not chastising those who are trying to help. They had no malicious intent. However, their fear of Me forced Me to take over, something I don't like to do when it involves the premature ending of a life.

As CC continued to examine her relationship with Me, she was constantly reminded that I can't be allowed to take lives because of fear or ineptitude and certainly not because of the egos of physicians who are more concerned with maintaining face than doing what's best for the patient. It's in these instances that CC has seen Me as the enemy, capitalizing on these human weaknesses and taking lives as collateral damage.

As CC has continued to practice medicine, she's come to see that we're partners. Instead of being angry, she's thankful when My presence frees a being from suffering or from an existence without hope or quality of life, even if the reason for this is inept care.

Chapter 3: Life Experiences as an Attending Physician

Question: What are some other observations You'd like to share with us?

Answer:

After being a resident and fellow, always under a watchful eye, CC could honestly say that when the day came that she was directly in charge of patients, she was scared and overwhelmed. She could no longer say, "Let me check with my attending." That person was her! And yes, even though there were other docs more senior than she to whom she could go with questions, it wasn't the same. They might render their opinions but, ultimately, the buck stopped with her, as the saying goes.

And so her adventures in life-and-death situations became even more intense. A baby could die because of a decision she made or because of her inability to provide a certain skill necessary to save its life. A wrong diagnosis or an incorrect treatment could alter a life forever or possibly terminate it. With that in mind, she began her career with the utmost respect for her responsibilities as a neonatologist, the guardian of the sickest and littlest of lives. As she came to discover, these responsibilities included not only saving lives but, at times, were expanded to taking care of the needs of patients' families.

As an attending, CC became the mediator in social situations that created hardships that might adversely affect a baby's life. She became a negotiator between payers and appropriate medical care, as well as assuring appropriate medical care, no matter the political milieu in which she was working. And finally, her role as an attending also evolved guiding families toward the decisions that needed to be made for their babies, even if that meant withdrawal of life support or placing the baby in palliative (hospice) care.

All these responsibilities are equally important not only to her but to every physician in order to provide the best medical care to all patients, especially patients entrusted to them by their loved ones. I was and always am with her and all physicians—ready to help, to ease suffering, and to be the pathway to freedom, if needed.

Of course, the role I take depends on how these responsibilities are handled by those physicians. I can tell you with certainty that I step in when I see half-hearted attempts to care for patients that lead to an untimely end. And, when I'm not respected as a necessary part of the treatment plan in some situations, all havoc can break loose. I'm relentless when I need to be to bring balance to the Universe.

Question: Talk about the times when humans have tried to deny You the ability to do Your job.

Answer:

This question should be asked more frequently within the medical community. As it happens, it is currently a topic of great interest. Therefore, I want to especially emphasize the following.

When I'm not allowed to do My job in appropriate situations, great suffering ensues.

There are many reasons that prevent Me to do My job in a timely fashion.
Patients or family members may refuse to allow withdrawal of life support. Some reasons may be religious, some may be selfishness in not wanting to let go, and some are simply born of fearing Me and the obvious finality I bring to life. In each situation in which I was fought from doing My job, the patient suffered tremendously and the outcome was the same—the patient eventually became My charge.

Furthermore, and more importantly, there are many physicians who also behave similarly and do everything in their power to prevent Me from taking a Soul that needs to come with Me. These situations are just as tragic, if not more so, because they hold the trust of families concerning the decisions that need to be made for their loved ones. If they cannot be honest with themselves and the families, the patients are left to experience "Death without dignity" and inevitably great suffering because of this. I return to the concept that CC teaches her students, "There are worse things than dying".

Allow Me to explain the above more clearly. Patients who are on life-support wouldn't survive without it. Sometimes this life-support is but a bridge to return to the living with reacquired health. But sometimes, this life-support cannot offer this option and it is these patients that need the honesty of the healthcare team to deliver this message to the families. When there is no hope for survival despite life-support being delivered, or whatever other extraordinary measures discussed to prolong life are offered, the discussion should always be honest as to what these treatments truly mean for the patient. In other words, if hope for survival, a survival that allows quality of life to be returned, is non-existent, then why prolong life just because the technology or medicines are available to do so? These are the patients that should be in My embrace. The greatest gift families can give those they love and whose possibility of a quality life has disappeared, is to let go. The greatest gift the healthcare team can give these patients and their families, is the honesty to discuss the futility of survival and the ability to give their loved ones the gift of "Death with dignity." It is during those times, all involved must see Me as their partner, providing their patients and/or loved one with peace from suffering. No matter what, I always eventually succeed when life can't continue. Whether the patient is hooked up to machines or not, whether the latest medicine or experimental treatment is given or not, I will do the job I need to, even if I am delayed. Just understand, this delay will cause increased suffering, that need not occur. Because to prolong the inevitable prevents Me from best serving the patient with "Death with Dignity".

CC has felt Me standing by her, patiently (or, sometimes, not so patiently) waiting, wishing I could take swift action and end that life. Unbelievably, I'm sometimes temporarily rendered powerless by those life-saving devices. Eventually, though, I'm able to do what I need to do.

The opposite can also happen. I've seen parents or other loved ones agree to withdrawal of life support only to have the patient take a few days or weeks to journey with Me, despite having no nutrition or medication. You might ask Me, "why does this happen? Why are families tortured for weeks, watching their loved ones slowly die in front of their eyes? What possible reason can there be for this scenario?" I can tell you with certainty that these patients do not suffer during this state. They still can feel the love the family has for them. Perhaps I can explain this by telling you the following. It allows the families to see their loved ones without all the tubes and machines previously used to keep them alive, thereby allowing their last memories to be of a time when their loved ones were not bound by technology. These situations aren't random. They're under the guidance of a Higher Source that understands the greatest love of all resides in every human and comprises compassion, humility, and grace.

Question: Tell us how You've angered healthcare workers, particularly physicians?

Answer:

My intent has never been and will never be, to anger healthcare workers. Simply, I've found that, for the most part, I'm ready to act if inappropriate care has been given, as I've stated before. Carelessness in medical decisions, ineptitude, and egos have all factored into adverse outcomes that can affect patients and their families forever. In these situations, I'm no one's partner but simply serve as a stark reminder of the consequence that poor care, for whatever reason, generates. No one can fight against Me in these instances because by the time these issues have been identified, it's too late for the patient. If you doubt that such events happen, think again.

To physicians, I suggest that the anger they feel toward Me when I take a patient that could have lived can be redirected toward respecting Me and having a better understanding of how you, as a medical professional, can prevent this from happening. The only way this can be done is through the best medical care you can provide to each and every one of your patients, devoid of politics, egos, carelessness, and overall stupidity. Only under these circumstances will I act appropriately. When the opposite is present, I'll act swiftly, without remorse and with the belief that by taking these patients into My care, I'm saving them from the additional suffering they'd experience at the hands of uncaring humans. It's up to you to figure out how to prevent these unnecessary scenarios from playing out for My benefit.

Let Me remind all of you that the human ego is a stubborn, powerful, all-or-nothing force that often causes poor decisions. When the ego is involved, all bets are off that the right thing will be done. That's My cue to take over, and take over I do. That is, after all, My nature. You see, I don't have an ego. I'm simply doing My job when others fail to do theirs.

Question: Have You been able to change lives by taking a loved one?

Answer:

There have been many times when My taking a loved one was a life-altering experience for their family. I remember one baby I took because of the mom's substance abuse while she was pregnant. After the baby passed into My care, CC was honest with this mother and told her that her baby's death was caused by her substance abuse and could have been prevented if she hadn't used drugs during her pregnancy. This mom left the hospital sad but mostly unresponsive to what CC had told her. CC believed nothing would change for this woman and that she'd probably see her again in the not-too-distant future in a similar scenario.

A few years later, this same mother returned to the nursery and CC hardly recognized her. She re-introduced herself and reminded her of what CC had told her that fateful day. She thanked CC for being brutally honest with her and told CC she'd immediately gotten help and had been clean for many months. She was now visiting juvenile detention facilities and talking to young girls about life and death and how they could make a difference in their lives. She was in a healthy relationship and was considering starting a family soon.

CC was so proud of her. She hugged her, knowing she'd be all right and her life would be great. Through CC, I positively affected this mom. Although I'd taken a life from her, I helped her turn her life around.

That day, CC and I had finally became true partners. We've had many more experiences together, and now always regard one another with respect.

Question: Any last thoughts before we move on?

Answer:

I love life. I exist because of life. My intention has never been to create sadness or hardship for those left behind. My role is one of a true facilitator. I facilitate passage into another place, another existence. I facilitate passage to meet the Creator of the Universe, the life-giving source of all living things, the Higher Source. Love is part of the nourishment the Universe provides, and I don't take this Love away. I simply redirect it back to the Creator of all that was, is, and forever will be.

Remember, life, as part of this love, can't be destroyed, ever. The Universe can't support the loss of even a molecule of this love. It supports everything, in all forms. Certainly, the finality I bring means physical separation and a perception of loss for those on this side of the veil, which causes much pain. For this, I'm truly sorry, but your time will come, and I promise to reunite you with those who have gone before you.

Please understand that I'm not bad or evil. Really. I wish the world wouldn't caricature Me as evil, dark, void of feeling, cold, and empty. If I could paint a picture of Myself, I'd be full of Light, for that's what I am. I'd be floating as angels do, not with wings but on the Love that the Universe constantly surrounds Me with. Around Me would be the essence of all the life I've taken with Me to a better place.

I believe CC has finally realized she shouldn't fear Me; that I was and continue to be her confidant, her partner, her assistant, so to speak, in the most complex of her cases. She finally realized how much she has and will always need Me, that I'm part of the natural process in her world. We're now old friends, tied by the bonds of Love and Life that can't be broken. Our experiences will continue to enrich this relationship.

I do know, too, that despite all the above, CC is still respectfully scared because, although she "sees" Me and "knows" what My true role is in the Universe, she hasn't personally met Me. Of course, that won't happen till it's her turn. Then I'll escort her with the same grace she showed to all her little ones and beloved pets. Her fear will melt away when she's reunited with all those who went before her and loved her dearly.

So you can better understand Me, the next part of this book tells the story of how I've been described through the ages and the latest theories concerning Me. Who knew I'd be considered so interesting!

I also wanted the opportunity to explain how I'm viewed relating to the loss of our animal companions. After all, animals are an important connection to our human existence in their ability to teach us about unconditional love, the purest love of all. Life is precious. All Life is precious. *All Life Is Precious.* Don't forget this, ever. *All Lives Matter!*

My intent in reviewing the history as well as the future of how I'm perceived is to try to dispel the negative, frightening images and ideas with which I've often been associated. As I've said before, I am Light, floating above the clouds, gentle and kind. Please try to see Me this way. If you can do this, each and every one of you will have an easier time when you meet Me, and you'll be filled with Love instead of fear. I promise.

PART 2: DEATH'S HISTORY

Chapter 1: The Cultural Perspective

Question: Please tell us how the ancient world viewed You and how that view has changed.

Answer:

I've been called many names throughout history. Perhaps My most favorite is Hades, which means the "unseen." I like this name because I prefer to be unseen rather than visualized as a dark, evil force. There is an alternate definition of Hades which I don't like. It comes from the Greeks, who portray Hades as the God of the Underworld, i.e., of the dead. Hades is also the name of the underworld I supposedly rule, a place described as dark, gloomy, misty, and full of Souls trapped in a nowhere land. Hades, in this literature, is a dark force to be feared.

The portrayal I like and which suits Me well, describes Me as escorting with patience and grace those passing to the next stage, making sure they don't get scared and lost. Remember, I can't help those whose life hasn't yet ended, those who are suffering with illness or the result of violent acts, but I can help the passage when the final moment has arrived, easing forever whatever pain they came from.

It must be the fear humans have always had about the seeming finality of what I bring that has caused My portrayals to be so unsavory.

In many depictions of Me, I'm relegated to the Underworld. Let Me be clear—this is *not* where I reside. I'm a partner of the Giver of Life and as such, a part of this beautiful Universe and the force that keeps it alive. The Underworld description implies that I'm inferior, lower than the dirt in which live the worms that decompose those who have died. Let Me state emphatically—that is NOT what I am. Remember, the body is but the vessel that carries the Soul.

Throughout time, My image, unfortunately, hasn't changed much—only My name. In art, I'm depicted as dark, skinny, skeletal, with a black robe and often riding a dark horse, sometimes with dark wings. Occasionally I'm depicted in feminine form, which is strange since it is the female that is the giver of life, but mostly I am depicted as a male. My eyes are often described as cavernous and bottomless, much like an abyss.

My earliest form appears in Neolithic paintings. In these, I'm a tall, pale, thin, winged being. I'd like all these images to be replaced by a sphere of Light, floating over those ready to come with Me on the journey. I want My image to bring feelings of warmth and comfort, not coldness and fear.

Another of My names, Azrael, was the most common name for Me in the early Judeo-Christian-Islamic world. Literally, this name means, "whom God helps" and, as such, is an integral part of the God Soul. Here I'm described appropriately as linked to Life, as part of the God Soul, which means God can't function without Me. Interestingly, the Romans called Me Pluto, which is related to the word for wealth. This seems to be more in relation to the wealth found in the life after death that I can bring to a person. These definitions and descriptions make sense to Me. They're truly who I am.

I know I'm feared because no one wants to leave their present life. That's human nature and the nature of all living things. I'm seen as "the" finality and linked with the unknown endpoint. Therefore, I believe the fear humans feel is caused as much by the unknown as by the perception that I represent the end of life.

Interestingly, in the ancient world, altars were made to Me, as Hades, to gain favor and assure a prominent place in the Underworld. As cultures evolved, no worshiping of Me has been documented. This is probably because of a belief that no amount of negotiating with Me, no prayers or sacrifices, would change My plan for each living being. Therefore, altars praising Me or supplicating Me would be for naught, even though My work is as important as the creation of Life.

What causes Me the most sadness is that I'm linked by some to Satan, or evil. I'm not associated with either. As the Creator of All has said, I am what I am. Nothing more, nothing less.
I'm most certainly associated with the Universe, the source of all Life.

One of the best tributes giving to Me came from Dion Fortune, who wrote in her 1942 book, *Through the Gates of Death,* the following:

"We must get out of the way of thinking that death is the ultimate tragedy... It is only the man sunk in matter who calls the Angel of Death the great enemy. His esoteric name is the Opener of the Gates of Life."

I like that. Opener of the Gates of Life. I'd add that these gates open to Eternal Life.

Throughout the ages, I've remained unchanged in imagery and as a source of fear. Most of the time, I'm the unwanted, unwelcome guest.

Perhaps, through this book, I can begin to be seen in a different way. Perhaps I can be seen as a messenger of Light, bringing the dead to the Light of Eternity, to a new existence, one without pain and suffering. Yes, I take the living from their loved ones, but this is only a temporary situation. Everyone will be reunited after his or her journey with Me to the next life. You'll find out what that is. I can't describe it, as it's impossible to describe using words. No one can explain where I will bring you.

Chapter 2: The Afterlife

Question: Where does the Soul go?

Answer:

Ah, where do I take you, you ask—the Hereafter, the Afterlife, Hades, the Last Judgment, Hell, Heaven, Purgatory, Limbo, or Reincarnation? There are so many names and so many descriptions that vary by the religious belief of each person. You can't talk about Me without wondering where you're going, where I'm taking you. So, what's the answer?

Let Me explain how the ancient religions view the Afterlife.

Egypt was well known for its depictions of life after death. It appears that their whole culture was based on their journey with Me. In fact, their society was based on Me, not on life.

Egyptians believed the Soul resided in the heart, which was deemed of utmost importance to preserve for the journey to be successful. Mummification was an important vehicle for delivery to the Afterlife. The Egyptians also believed that I only created a temporary interruption of life. I didn't bring an individual to a final destination but to the beginning of Life Eternal. To successfully achieve this, the whole body had to be preserved, hence the need for mummification.

The Egyptians had it partially right. I didn't bring finality to life but rather Life Eternal. To be Egyptian meant that life didn't end when the last breath was taken but continued on in a different form and in a different place. I wasn't so much the messenger or guide as I was the actual realm in which the Soul came to reside. For the Egyptians, I was bigger than a deity. I was actually the Afterlife personified. The error the Egyptians made was to make Me more important than Life. There must be a balance, a ying/yang, so to speak, when I'm compared to the Giver of Life on earth.

In Greece and in Rome, as I've previously described, I was known as Hades, the god of the Underworld, the guide that lead Souls across a river into a land that bears my name. The Soul would then be judged on its merits and assigned a realm based on those merits. There were four different lands where Souls could land. Elysium was for those Souls that had lived a pure life. Tartarus was for those that blasphemed against the gods and were rebellious and/or evil. The Asphodel Fields housed a variety of Souls whose evil deeds equaled their good deeds as well as Souls who, for whatever reason, hadn't yet been judged. Finally, the Fields of Punishment were for those Souls who had sinned, but not as badly as those that were sent to

Tartarus. The Afterlife beliefs of the Greeks and the Romans were similar.

In the present, the religions that currently exist continue to contain some of these ancient beliefs. Perhaps there was little new information throughout history to answer the ancient question, "What happens when I die?" In any case, little has changed to help you understand and cope with the finality you all believe I bring.

I'd like to state, for the record, that your belief system of what the Afterlife is like, will be what you'll encounter after I take you with Me. In other words, each person's description of the Afterlife is neither right or wrong. To have it one way or another would bring great discomfort to a Soul with a different belief. My journey with your Soul isn't about discomfort but about reuniting you with the Universe in a place of Light, Knowledge, and Love. Therefore, this journey must be one free of fear, distrust, and angst despite its unfamiliarity. On the contrary, it must be a journey that mirrors the belief system of each individual Soul. Those who believe in reincarnation will have the opportunity to choose their next life to do the repair work needed. Those who have a different belief will be gently brought to a state of renewal, where repair work can be done and where they'll also be given the opportunity to choose to re-enter life wherever that may bring them to do the repair work needed.

The exception to this concerns those who believe that there will be a prize given in the afterlife for deeds done that are believed to bring honor to the Higher Source. I can clearly state for you, there is no prize, no compensation, physical or otherwise, for any perceived honor you feel you have brought to the Universe. Those sentiments are human and only of human origin, without basis for the holiness that the Higher Source, Was, Is and Will be forever. The only honor that you can give to the Universe, is to live your life to the fullest, bestowing love and compassion to the world around you and honoring each breath as a gift from the Universe.

The end point of your life, of course, is the reunion of your Soul with Light, Love, and the Knowledge of the Universe, no matter how you get there, how long it takes, or to what "lands" you visit. It is the basic right of each Soul to be reunited with the Universe. But, be forewarned, that right can be stripped if the Soul has traded the values given by the Universe for those made by humanity falsely to honor the Universe.

I will not describe each current religion's belief, however. You know what you believe in and so to further describe other religions would not do those religions earthly justice, since their individual theologies can not be summarized for simplicity's sake.

Nor do I want to insult any reader with My denial that your particular belief is wrong. That is for your Soul to learn and accept on it's own terms.

Instead, let Me be very clear, once again, so there is no confusion, as to where I will take your Soul.

I will take your Soul to a place within the Universe where knowledge and love will repair and allow that Soul to progress. There are exceptions, however. Simply put, there are Souls that cannot be repaired. These are the Souls that are broken beyond repair and will be destroyed by the Higher Source so their ability to harm can no longer be allowed. It does not matter what religion that Soul belonged to. No religion will be protected from this Eternal Law. Men may think they know what happens. They do not. Again, do not be fooled by those among you that proclaim their assurances of any sort of compensation for deeds done in the name of the Higher Source. They are all false. To listen to these lies can imperil your Soul to the Truth of what the Higher Source has planned. Be vigilant. I speak the truth for the Higher Source.

Question: Can You please talk about science as it relates to You and the nature of the Soul? In fact, some people refer to science as another religion.

Answer:

What is science, but the Creation by the All-Knowing? Yet, science is now competing with religions to better explain the unexplainable. To some, science is a valid religion because it's based on fact and not on belief systems. Modern science tries to prove or disprove theories and, because of this, I've been subjected to a world of experiments to prove My existence.

It's obvious that I'm real. I, Death happen to every living organism on this planet. What becomes scientifically difficult to examine is what happens after Life ceases. What happens to the consciousness of a person after death? Is the definition of consciousness the same as the definition of the Soul? Are they one in the same?

Let Me put forth the theories currently being touted as possibilities. According to Dr. Stuart Hameroff, Professor Emeritus at the Departments of Anesthesiology and Psychology and the Director of the Center of Consciousness Studies at the University of Arizona, and Sir Roger Penrose, a theoretical physicist, consciousness actually resides in microtubules within brain neurons and is regulated by the laws of quantum physics. As such, when a body dies, the electric energy contained in these microtubules are released into the Universe to migrate as a Soul entity. The next question is, "Where do these Souls, as described above, go?"

Apparently, there's been much criticism of this particular theory, specifically questions about where this energy within these microtubules goes, for what purpose, and to what final destination. Remember what Albert Einstein taught you: Energy cannot be created or destroyed.

I can state with confidence that the theory presented above has some truth to it. That is, the concept of what consciousness is and its description as residing within brain cells is true. It's these thought connections that make up the Soul of a person and guides that person in their daily deeds of good, evil, or in between. However, this theory doesn't apply after the person dies. Yes, the energy of each consciousness is released into the Universe, but it's released as a whole entity. I help it to travel to the realm of Wisdom, Love, and Light.

It's during the Soul's travels that it reunites with other Souls with whom it had intimate contact in earthly life. It's within these relationships that the journey becomes easier.

Let me further complicate the discussion by describing

to you one of the most recent theories about the Soul, which is presented by Robert Lanza, M.D. It's called Biocentrism. Dr. Lanza states, "Although individual bodies are destined to self-destruct, the alive feeling—the 'Who am I?'—is just a 20-watt fountain of energy operating in the brain. But this energy doesn't go away at death. One of the surest axioms of science is that energy never dies; it can neither be created nor destroyed. But does this energy transcend from one world to the other?"

His answer is yes; it exists in alternate universes.

Similar to the previous discussion of consciousness residing in microtubules and being released after death, Lanza's theory describes consciousness as a "20-watt fountain of energy" that goes on to exist in another universe.

In the end (no pun intended), it doesn't matter what theory you believe regarding the nature of the Soul, consciousness, or whatever you want to call the nonphysical part of yourselves that continues after the death of the body. What's true is that this energy isn't destroyed. It evolves, and I help it in its travels.

Essentially, think of Me as the final Travel Agent, standing at the ready when your physical body ceases to exist to take the essence of who you truly are—your Soul—to a place of Light, Learning, and pure Love.

Of course, the fear that you the reader feels also consumes all living things and derives from letting go of the known for the unknown. In other words, leaving a physical existence that's known, even though at times it's filled with pain, suffering, and agony, both physical and mental, is hard when your travel will take you to the unknown. That unknown, to which your Soul travels and finally rests, is what's so disturbing to most. This unknown, including the fear that perhaps there might not be anything beyond life but nothingness, a black empty void, is what has created My image as dark, sinister, evil, and unrelenting. Within this fear, I become the taker of life, a greedy, uncaring persona whose aim is to destroy happiness and replace it with sorrow.

Yet, after all I've told you, both through CC's experiences and via different beliefs systems, ancient and current, isn't the opposite obvious? Shouldn't you see Me as the Messenger of Light that will take you to a place where you reunite with other Souls and become one with the Universe?

I would like it—very much—if this becomes the image you see when you hear My name. Although there's sorrow in saying goodbye to a loved one in this lifetime, to know that, through Me, you'll be reunited with their Soul in the not-too-distant future should bring you great comfort.

PART 3: THE MANY FACES OF DEATH

Chapter 1: Suicide

Question: I'd like to ask You about some controversial topics. The first is suicide. What happens to a Soul released through suicide?

Answer:

I am who I am. I am Light, I am one with the Universe, and I am the full, equal partner of the Higher Source. I assist the Higher Source by taking the Spirit to a new plane.

I don't take away life, I don't kill, and I don't end a life prematurely just because I want to. As I have said before, any given life may end prematurely because of other humans, but not because of My desire to do so. I'm not evil. I'm not in league with the devil. I don't intend to wreck havoc.

These concepts are important for humans to understand when they think or talk about Me. It's also important to discuss these topics, which cause so much pain and fear in humanity, so I'm seen not as the cause of suffering but as the means to bring Love and Light to all Souls.

So, let's begin with suicide. Suicide is an unnatural ending of a life given by the Universe. This life isn't bestowed randomly, therefore taking one's life before it's natural end is tragic. It saddens the Universe. It saddens Me. I'm involved only to guide that troubled Soul to a place to reflect, to understand the gravity of the decision taken, and to reboot that Soul, so to speak, so it will be ready for re-entry into life again.

There are many reasons that humans commit suicide. All involve desperation and depression, where the perception of the next day brings no relief. It's the last act of a human at the end of the road, emotionally, physically, and spiritually.

There have been and continue to be many forms of suicide: mass suicides, double suicides involving a sick spouse whose partner can't live without them, and individual suicides in cases of terminal illnesses, the influence of drugs, or severe depression. In each instance, the feeling of desperation arises from not believing there's any other alternative.

From a historical perspective, when the earliest mass suicides are evaluated, you see they were really "mercy killings" of a group of people to avoid torture, abuse, or being taken as slaves by the enemy. One of the best-known incidents took place in Masada in AD 73, where 967 Jewish men, women, and children lived after the Romans destroyed Jerusalem. All but two women and five children died there. The rest took their lives to escape a life that was untenable to them. I was there to lead those Souls to the greater light, to rejoin the Universe of Love and Tolerance.

There are also mass suicides that occur secondary to a deranged leader telling the group he or she leads that they'll be going to a better place after death. These leaders aren't sane and their followers are misled. Such leaders are, in fact, mass murderers. Nonetheless, the followers who gave up their lives were taken to a place of great Love and Wisdom, shown their error in judgment, and cleansed in the Light of the Universe.

The most common question I'm asked regarding suicide is, what happens to these Souls? Are they punished? Are they relegated to an Afterlife of torment and hate?
As the Travel Guide for all Souls, I can say without doubt this is not the case. Suicide isn't murder. Suicide is sad for those left behind, but it brings rest for the Soul whose body had been wracked by pain, disease, or mental suffering. The Universe doesn't consider suicide a cowardly act. A Soul that's released from its body through suicide is treated with great gentleness and care. It's a Soul in need of much Love and Light and therefore is immediately bathed in the infinite Light and

Love of the Universe. After it repairs itself, it's released to be reborn in the physical world, to succeed and help others learn a better way.

I understand that many of you reading this will be in complete disagreement with what I've just said. What I'm telling you transcends any religious theory or dogma. Let Me further explain. The rules and dogmas of every world religion are all man-made. I understand that many of you reading this believe the "holy books" you hold dear to your particular religious' beliefs were written or somehow transmitted to a certain chosen few, by the Higher Source. Although, there may be Divine Intervention in some ancient texts, the Universe has no use for artificial rules presented to humankind by other humans devoid of Divine Intervention. They were created by men to wield power over others. Also, the interpretation of these "holy laws" further complicate the natural laws the Higher Source hoped would be adopted by humans. Yes, you were and are created in the image of the Higher Source. That image refers to the Soul, not the physical characteristics. Within that Soul, the "laws" given pertain to the entire Universe and are centered in Universal Love, Compassion and Understanding. Therefore, as an example, the law called a commandment, of "Thou Shall Not Kill", pertains in the taking away the Soul's right to exist. It does not pertain to physically killing another. That does not mean anyone can go around physically killing others because they do not act like you do, believe like you do, or for whatever selfish reason you feel a life can be taken. Thou Shall Not Kill pertains to preventing a Soul, connected to a body, being taken for selfish, unloving and non-compassionate reasons. As an example, beheading another because they are "religious infidels" and therefore justified, goes against what the Higher Source ever intended. Assisting a Soul to be released from a body racked with disease, is not considered killing by the Higher Source. It is the interpretation by human minds that have called it murder. I can apply this to any "law" human believe to be "divine" and show that the human interpretation, is just that, human. The "laws" are divine, but because they are interpreted in a "human" fashion, they lose their divine spark and become solely "man-made". We will examine the fundamental 10 laws called by most, the ten commandments, in more depth further on. I want to explain to you what the Higher Source intends for humanity to understand. This will help you all understand My role within the Universe and My partnership with the Higher Source.

Therefore, regarding the topic of suicide, the Universe, the Higher Source, the Alpha and the Omega, whatever your name is for the Ultimate Love and Wisdom that exists into infinity, understands that the abrupt end of a physical life doesn't end the Soul of that being. Instead, the Universe helps heal it and redirects it into the physical realm, as I stated above.

I say to those of you who've lost a loved one to suicide, please don't despair. Although you once knew that person as tortured mentally, or in physical pain, that person's Spirit, once released to Me, is taken to the ultimate "spa" of the Universe, a place where only the greatest care is given to restore that Soul to its original purity.

However each Soul comes to be with Me—as the result of illness, suicide, murder, or natural causes—I have the opportunity to communicate with that Soul. Those that come to Me through suicide have much to tell. Each and every one of those Souls regrets their final act. They tell Me about the reasons that led to this action, and then they tell Me how sad they are for the people who loved them and are now left behind. Every one of these Souls tells Me that those around them aren't responsible for their death. Even those who commit suicide because they were abused don't blame those who acted so poorly toward them. These Souls understand it was their inability to see the goodness in others, in the Universe, and in the power of Life and Love that caused them to take their life. The catalyst may have been the abuse, but it wasn't the true cause.

My final words for those left behind is to continue to have faith in the Universe and to believe its infinite Love and Wisdom can be tapped at any time. The familiar statement, "Ask and you shall receive" is very true. The energy source of all creation is powerful. Ask it to take care of your loved one and bring that Soul peace. As you ask this, know it has already come to pass.

Chapter 2: Euthanasia

Question: What about euthanasia? Does the Universe consider it compassion or is it considered murder?

Answer:

I'm present at the end of every life, whether the cause of its cessation is natural or not. I'm not a judge. As I have stated before, I am the guide for all Souls to return to the Universe.

By human standards, euthanasia is controversial, often more so than suicide, because it involves taking the life of another person by essentially being an accomplice in ending the life of that person. Much of the human controversy centers around the potential for the slippery-slope argument. This means that the determination of who's qualified to decide when another's life should end can be tricky. A desire to take over the dying person's estate, resentment about the inconvenience of taking care of the ill person, or simply not liking that person are some of the possible motivations that may come into play in decisions about ending a life. Even if a person asks to be euthanized, what if they're no longer deemed competent to make that decision for themselves, and who decides such competency?

Many would consider euthanasia to be another form of suicide—assisted suicide—and, as such, a crime against the Giver of Life and, therefore, murder. There are many works by theologians, philosophers, and ethicists as well as those in the medical community that discuss this topic and make judgments as to what's right or wrong. As an example, in Judaism, it's widely understood that "if the choice is between life or death, choose life." Another saying is, "Where there's life, there's hope." However, this advice is designed to counteract the ancient traditions of martyrdom and human sacrifice. Therefore, it doesn't apply to situations such as euthanasia. You can't consider these sentiments as inherently part of the argument for or against so-called mercy killing. In fact, it's humans, not the Higher Source, that create the arguments for or against euthanasia. Therefore, any argument brought forth is immediately faulty, as it relies solely on human thought and perceptions, which naturally carry human biases.

Let Me further examine this point. If the argument is that holy writings state that suicide or euthanasia is considered to be a sin against the All-Knowing, how can you explain condoning genocide of a whole population to avenge one death or to achieve a particular political goal? Examples include David killing 200 Philistines so he could take Michal, King Saul's daughter, for his wife.

Consider as well the description of God commanding His people to eradicate a population because they don't worship Him or keep His commandments. Isn't all of creation part of God's work? Are not all living things worthy of Love, Compassion, and Forgiveness?

Let Me reiterate. Referencing "holy" writings to give credence to arguments against suicide or euthanasia do not hold up because there's no credibility that these words were derived from an all-knowing, all-loving Higher Source. Therefore, those who request euthanasia and those that help them accomplish this aren't judged but instead are assisted by the Higher Source, as long as the motivation of all involved is truly altruistic and not based on selfishness in any form.

Like suicide, then, euthanasia is considered by the Universe as a means of delivering a Soul tortured by illness or pain to the Universe where it can be healed. That Soul travels with Me in great relief and comfort, knowing that this journey leads to a restoration of wholeness.

To those who've assisted another in this passage because either they loved that person so much or were medically trained and knew that Soul needed to pass to a better place I say, "You're a blessed person." To any that request help to pass on to a better place, be assured I'll always be there to assist you in your travels. You, too, are blessed, for your Soul requests to be whole again through the Universe. The Universe doesn't want any living form to suffer. There is love enough for all.

Regarding the euthanasia of our animal companions, you see that, for the most part, there's little to no ethical difficulty providing relief of suffering at the end of a beloved pet's life. Why are your feelings so different regarding humans? Do you believe that animals don't have a Soul? Is that why these decisions are easier? Did the same Source of All Knowledge and Light that created you not create them?

Do you believe animals don't feel grief? They may not cry, but they demonstrate their sorrow in other ways. In fact, you have it well documented that in the wild, animals respond to the death of one of their own with displays of grief and sorrow. These displays include but are certainly not limited to the following. Elephants will hold vigils over a dead family member, as well as attempt to resuscitate one of their own. Wolves will stop howling and instead produce a slow mournful cry at the death of a pack member. Primates will slowly file past their dead friend and sniff the body as if to say their final goodbyes. A Llama will sometimes die within a day after its mate dies, because the loss is too much for the survivor. Even magpies respond to the death of a member of their family by creating a chorus of cackles that resonates through the woods and is echoed by another distant chorus of cackles from other magpies.

Grief, love, and happiness are emotions felt by all living things, according to their capacity. Non-human, animal Souls aren't as complex as human Souls. Instead they are more a collective essence of Light and Love given by the Universe and are indeed more than sufficient to connect to the Higher Source. Don't underestimate the beauty of the Creator and the Creation.

Chapter 3: War, Violent Acts, Disease, Catastrophic Natural Events, and Other Human Situations that Dictate When I'm Needed

Question: The reader would be interested in the explanation of Your relationship to war and violence.

Answer:

First, let Me tell you that the Universe is crying, constantly crying. The wars that ravage whole populations and destroy nations, communities, and races in your world horrify the Universe. Among many examples, there's the destruction of countless lives wrought by the Inquisition; the Final Solution, which the Nazis used to great effect; and, more recently, the chemical warfare that's killed innocent children and women. These are but a small sample of the sordid human history of killing for so many ridiculous reasons.

I know that many of you wonder how I can be in so many places at one time, since your methods kill thousands—sometimes hundreds of thousands—so quickly. I'm not one entity. I'm part of the Light and Love of the Universe and, as such, I'm everywhere at once. Remember, I'm part of the Universe, a partner with the Higher Source, and part of the Godhead or God Soul, present everywhere, always. The Higher Source brings life to all living things, and I take that life and return it to the Light and Love of the Universe.

My greatest sorrow is the pain experienced by humans in these tragic, man-made situations. These aren't peaceful deaths but deaths involving much pain and mental agony as people are ripped from their lives before they're ready. I guide them when they pass and help to ease their pain as they travel to a place that instantly heals.

Question: Why are children allowed to suffer so? It seems impossible to come up with any possible reason.

Answer:

Such horrific deaths... I cannot describe the terror in a child's Soul before it's tortured or killed as part of the worldwide human trafficking that occurs in the sex and slave trades. I am witness to countless children who are physically and verbally abused. Pedophiles that prey on innocent lives also bring a great deal of sorrow to the Universe. These are some of the worst evils created by and performed by humans against humans.

When children die, I'm the gentlest spirit as I accompany these innocents and present Myself as the brightest Light, full of intense warmth. I surround them with so much love that their terror instantly disappears as they're taken to a place of protection against all that is evil in the world. The Universe embraces these children's Souls with great tenderness. Their suffering dissipates forever. They don't return to a life on earth. They go to another life, in another realm, where they never experience suffering again.

In other situations, Souls are taken early not because it was that Soul's destiny but because the medical help was wanting or the physical situation couldn't support life. Again, these cases, as in the the horrific deaths described above, occur because there's a clear human choice involved, whether it be by an individual, a community or a government. It is never a decision made by the Higher Source. In all of these cases, each Soul is wrapped in warmth, Love, and the Universe's promise to never allow that Soul to suffer again.

Children who die because of medical reasons, unable to be healed by your methods, also are taken to a place of great Love, Compassion and Healing light, where their Souls will be free from any form of suffering.

Question: It seems You're becoming increasingly present these days, especially in man-made disasters that were either caused by an intent to harm or through carelessness. Why does the Higher Source allow innocents to suffer and die?

Answer:

The examples of man-made death are abundant. The fire in the clothing factory in Pakistan that killed so many wasn't a choice made by the Higher Source. It was a choice of humans who allowed working conditions to be dangerous so garments could be manufactured and sold at a fraction of what they'd cost if they were made under conditions that were safe.

The lives lost secondary to flooding because levies broke weren't random or an act of the Higher Source. These casualties were caused by humans who didn't want to spend money to upgrade the levies to be strong enough to contain flood waters.

The death of more than three thousand people at the hands of terrorists on 9/11/01 wasn't the plan of the Higher Source but the consequence of anger in those who perpetrated these horrific crimes.

Perhaps you also wonder why some people die young or good people are taken away too early despite all the beneficial work they do. Why is a missionary killed when a murderer gets away with his crime? What sense is there in a newborn baby dying soon after birth despite its mother doing everything right during the pregnancy while a baby born to a mother who took drugs during the entire pregnancy survives?

I can't explain these things to you. I can tell you there's a higher plan for your Souls, but that's all I can say. Such knowledge is for the Higher Source to reveal to each Soul, through Me, after it passes from its human existence. To attempt to explain this to a human during its life on earth would be impossible, since a human relies on its five senses to understand its physical world. Any explanation I give wouldn't make sense and would be dismissed as science fiction.

So yes, although there's a plan for each of you as to the time your Soul journeys with Me, there are many instances where the free choice of humans supersedes the plans of the Higher Source. You might think, "Wow, humans can change what the Higher Source has planned for each and every one of us"? The answer is complicated. Your Souls were given free-choice as part of the human experience. Free-choice allows each Soul, while earthbound, to operate without intervention from the Higher Source. In fact, the prayers each Soul sends to the Higher Source are part of that Soul's "fine-tuning" so to speak, of their free choice. A prayer that was "answered" was not because the Higher Source listened and did what was asked, but rather it was because of that Soul's attachment to the Universe. In other words, this attachment allowed the Universe to be "tweaked" so that that particular prayer could be answered. Sometimes, prayers cannot be answered as a particulr Soul would want. But never think that any prayer or supplication is not heard and/or not answered. The answer may simply be different than what the Soul had wanted. The answer, however different than expected, will always be correct for that Soul and/or the Souls involved. Once the Soul leaves the confines of earth and travels to be closer to the Higher Source, this concept will be instantaneously understood. The physical confines of the Soul's existence make it very difficult to explain this with any more clarity. As humans, I understand you want to have complete understanding now. However, the complexity of this understanding, which supersedes the five senses, won't be revealed to you until your Soul is ready for the next journey.

Question: Why don't You take newborns who are destined for a life of suffering? And what happens to the souls of unbaptized babies?

Answer:

As I mentioned in the last chapter, many ask Me, "Why don't You take those that You know will have a life of suffering? Why allow them to live a life full of pain—physical as well as emotional?" Again, let Me be clear. I do NOT choose whom to take. I follow the Higher Source's plan in taking a Soul on the journey to a place of Light, Love, and Healing. There are reasons why some are taken early, others suffer throughout life, and others are taken quickly so as not to suffer.

In the case of babies that die soon after birth and have no chance to have the human ritual of baptism, don't worry. These sweet Souls don't go to hell, as some would have you believe. The Universe accepts these Souls joyfully and takes them to a place where they choose to re-enter life as a human or go to another plane where further learning can take place in other ways. Remember, the ritual is human, not created by the Universe.

Those children who live a life full of suffering, have Souls who have chosen that human life to learn lessons needed to continue to evolve closer to the Higher Source.

Question: What about deaths caused by natural catastrophe?

Answer:

The same applies to those that die in catastrophic natural disasters—earthquakes, tornados, and tsunamis, for example. Agony is part of this death process, but I'm able to ease the passage of each person.

Many have asked why these disasters occur. Just as the Universe has no control over human actions, it doesn't control natural disasters or diseases. It can only cry in despair for all the beautiful, innocent lives taken too early, because the full potential of those lives will never be realized. If I could teach you anything during your lives, it's to appreciate every moment of life, not only yours but that of all who surround you, whether they're your family or friends or not. In fact, every living being of all species deserves life and the freedom to enjoy every moment to its fullest.

CRISTINA CARBALLO-PERELMAN, M.D.

Question: You've spoken several times about animals. How do You feel about the killing of animals to feed humans?

Answer:

Thank you for asking this. It's an important question. Animals have an essence, or simple Soul, that's part of the Universe and, as such, they deserve Light and Love as much as you do. Although it's hard for many of you to hear, the Universe doesn't sanction the killing of animals to feed humans, especially when such slaughter is also for the purpose of profit and there's no concern for the pain and agony these animals experience—not only at the time they're slaughtered but throughout their lives. Humans can live without animal protein, and, in fact, as science has explained, diets devoid of animals are much healthier than those containing the flesh of other beings. It's easy for humans to forget that what's on their dinner plate was once a life with its own essence, a Soul-like energy, and the capacity for joy, all given to it by the Universe. Humans have no right to take those lives for personal enjoyment. Many may quote the writings found in books human call their "holy" books, books that state man has dominion over all other living things on this earth. That doesn't mean humans own those lives and can take them at will. That isn't what the Universe wants. You, as humans, were given free will, free choice and intelligence. This was given to you explicitly to bring healing to the world, not death.

In conclusion, there's much misery in the world. You have asked Me to discuss the wars of men, the tragic natural disasters that take so many lives, and the countless animals that are inhumanely slaughtered to satisfy humans' carnivorous cravings or for the sheer thrill of the hunt. I hope that I have been able to convey My angst concerning the taking of the the Souls involved. However, the important message to take away from My discussion, is that despite the tragedy involved, each Soul is treated with great care. The journey I take each Soul on is always bathed in Warmth, Light and Love. All the animals I take with me, who have not been partially imbued with a human's Soul, are returned to the Higher Source as part of Light and Love. Animals that have been loved by humans, have been given a special gift, a part of the human Soul that loved it, as I will explain further on. These animals are returned to the Universe and reunited with that human Soul.

Chapter 4: Abortion

Question: This is a tough and controversial issue. Is an abortion considered to be the murder of an innocent Soul? If it isn't, can You tell us when does life begin?

Answer:

First of all, life never begins or ends. It always is. The Soul attaches itself to a human body when that body enters the external world from the internal world, the womb. Remember My discussion of the Soul being contained within the microtubules of the brain? The Soul attached to a human body needs experience and memory. It can't exist without these. At the death of fetus, the departed Soul that was to be a part of that human, takes its energy and joins the Light of the Universe to learn lessons, grow, evolve, and be healed. Though the Soul exists, it can only manifest itself while on earth within a human, i.e. when there's an external physical world to experience. Please understand, the Soul can also exist elsewhere in the Universe in different forms, gathering experiences in whatever realm it is in. However, in your human world, it requires a human body. Therefore, a Soul may tentatively attach itself to a fetus developing in the uterus, but it's not fully associated with that body until birth.

Murder pertains to the taking of a human life that has a Soul. In your world, killing an animal isn't considered murder because a non-human isn't considered to have a Soul. Therefore, abortion isn't considered murder because the Soul hasn't yet attached itself to the fetus.

The Soul of the mother who allowed her fetus to be aborted, for whatever reason, however, will need to have significant reparation after her own physical death, to heal the feelings of guilt and sadness she may feel as a result of her decision to terminate the process of a Soul attempting to attach itself to a developing human body.

Humanity has tried to answer this question within a religious context. In an attempt to be perceived as "merciful", many of your religious doctrines do not condemn abortions done in an effort to save the life of the mother or in cases where the fetus is malformed and unable to survive after birth or when the fetus is a product of rape, incest or even when a mother is deemed ill-equipped to raise a child. However, in all these cases, a human life was developing and a Soul was attaching itself to the fetus. Therefore, it doesn't matter what the human reasons are for terminating a particular pregnancy. In the end, the connection of that particular Soul with the developing human body was severed. Please understand, that the Universe, does not consider these situations as murder because the developing fetus didn't yet have a Soul permanently attached.

You might ask, "What about babies who are killed within hours of being born because they're unwanted?" It is true that those babies would have minimal memories, yet the Soul would be permanently attached. In other words, after the first independent breath, the Soul belongs to that human body. Memories begin to be created in that particular life and the union is sealed. At that moment and afterward, killing that newborn is considered murder.

The next question, "When does life actually begin?" is easier to understand with the following answer. Remember, life, in terms of a Soul, does not begin or end. Physical life, however, begins with the union of the sperm and egg. However, the union of the Soul with that physical being doesn't become permanent until the first breath the baby takes after the umbilical cord is severed. At that moment, a human becomes a person, not just a physical being.

Human life, as defined by the Universe, requires a Soul. All other living things exist as part of the Universe and contain the essence of the Universe, but they don't have Souls. The ability to feel emotions doesn't mean a being has a Soul. Animals certainly feel, but the Soul is a special addition to humans, along with free choice, given by the Higher Source.

There's one exception to this that I'll subsequently discuss. This exception occurs when a human loves an animal. When that happens, part of that human's Soul attaches to that animal. More on this concept later

Question: Do babies who are born with severe disabilities that affects normal brain development have a Soul?

Answer:

By asking Me this question, you are assuming that if a human is not "normal" it does not have a Soul. You could not be more incorrect in your thinking.

The error is believing that the Soul requires full brain function as we know it, to exist.

The Soul exists within a body whether it is disabled, physically or mentally or not. In the case of mental disabilities at all ages, the Soul is as much a part of that person as someone without mental disabilities. This includes mental illnesses such as psychosis, schizophrenias, anxiety disorders, manic-depressive disorders and onward. It also includes babies born with brain disorders that significantly affect learning. Remember the Soul enters a particular body to learn lessons needed to continue to evolve and move on. The feelings, senses and thoughts, no matter how simple or disturbed allows the Soul to learn it's lessons within that environment or may in fact be present within a disabled person to enable it to teach other Souls how to care and respect for others with these disabilities.

Therefore, do not discount those around you with significant disabilities, their Souls require the same compassion, love, tolerance and teaching as anyone else.

In the process of helping those who require assistance, your Soul may be positively impacted very significantly.

You must remember that Souls belong to bodies, but are not disabled like those bodies or minds. These Souls are whole and fully functioning within the constraints those bodies and/or minds present.

Chapter 5: Dementia

Question: OK, You just answered what happens to those Souls trapped in a body with mental disease. What if the Soul resides in the mind or brain, where dementia or coma sets in? Is the Soul trapped or is it taken by You to another place as, or before the body dies?

Answer:

It's been exceptionally hard for humans to understand that the Soul is truly a separate entity from the body it inhabits. During your lifetime on earth, the two function as a unit, but never forget that the Soul is a totally separate entity that uses the body as a means to be both a teacher and a student. If you, as a human, can grasp this concept, you can begin to understand that the mind is merely a vehicle for the Soul to inhabit to attain the goals it came to earth to accomplish. Therefore, when the mind or brain begins to deteriorate because of dementia, the Soul escapes but does not flee. In other words, it hovers close by, under My care, waiting for the body to die. I can't take the Soul away from the living body, even though the brain is no longer able to communicate with it and be its "eyes and ears," so to speak. The pact is made at birth that until the physical body ceases to exist, the Soul can't abandon it. Life isn't defined only by a beating heart but by the presence of the Soul, whether it be within the body or hovering nearby, waiting for its release.

You might ask, "Why would the Soul leave the body and hover? Why not leave completely or stay inside the body until it dies?" Once the mind has lost the ability to be the circuit board for the Soul, its function is finished. Although the Soul can't abandon the body completely, it also can't stay inside a mind affected with dementia because to do so would impair the Soul's identity. It would be like a corrupt program on a computer wiping out the files. Although the Soul travels through time and space and is eternal, it's also fragile and can be easily corroded if left inside a mind that's losing function. Remember, this is different than a Soul that is within a body with a mental disability, as I discussed previously. Those Souls chose to enter a body whose mind was plagued with illness or disabilities, even if the mental illness started later in life.

To return to our present discussion, the same holds true for a person who's comatose or where brain activity is gone or in the process of shutting down. In all these cases, the Soul will exit and hover, waiting for the final release so I can escort it to its next stop.

I'm sure you've read or heard stories about people who've had near-death experiences in which they describe hovering over their bodies, watching as heroic measures are taken to bring them back to life. Comatose patients who recover sometimes relay what they heard people in their hospital room saying to or about them while they were unconscious. These experiences are real. They're the experiences the Soul has as it hovers near its physical body.

So, yes, although a patient with dementia or in a coma appears not to know what's happening around them, the Soul of that person is ever present and aware of the love and caring that others are providing to that "person."

Here are My final words on this particular topic: Don't abandon the person who appears to be unresponsive because of a brain malfunction, whether it be caused by dementia or injury. Continue to communicate with them. Show them how much they're loved. Their Soul continues to listen and feel until the last breath is taken. Remember, even after physical death, the Soul will forever remember the Love it received. This is because it's not just another person giving or showing that Love, it's another Soul. As Souls, you'll all reconnect once you're free of your physical forms.

PART 4: THE END IS ONLY THE BEGINNING

Chapter 1: Who I Really Am

Question: What can be done to change the negative image that humans have of You? Have any seen You in a positive light?

Answer:

My role is to ensure the Soul doesn't become lost on its journey to the Higher Source. This is the critical understanding that will allow humans to see Me as an assistant to that Source, not the evil culprit that steals lives and spirits the Soul to some dark and dreary underworld.

Thankfully, not all see Me as evil incarnate. There are cultures around the world that actually "honor" me. I've explained to you the dark, creepy, evil characteristics that have been used to describe me. I've also talked about the persona given to Me by the living throughout the centuries. Now I'm going to show you how I'm honored by some cultures, maybe because of fear, but I prefer to think it's because these cultures understand that I'm not the cause of the cessation of life.

The best celebrations of Me were begun by the ancient indigenous cultures of the Aztecs and Mayans. These celebrations honored Me and continue to honor Me with food and effigies representing death. The most common figures used today for this purpose in Mexico and many other Latin cultures is the decorated skull or skeleton. Death in this culture isn't feared but rather revered as an intermediary in communication with those who have left this life and are able to guard the living, protect them, and bring good fortune.

Unfortunately, not all current traditions honor Me. In some traditions, the body is regarded as the Temple of the Soul, and the belief is that it should be protected and maintained for as long as possible. Therefore, I'm considered "persona non grata," so to speak. I'm the unwelcome guest because I take the Soul from the body.

However, please understand, the Soul never belonged to that body. The body is only a vessel, a vehicle to accomplish its task here on earth. That vessel dies, but the Soul doesn't. Consider a flower vase. When empty, it's inanimate. Add water and flowers and you have a living entity. If the vase breaks, the flowers don't disappear. They remain and are placed in another vase (another body).

In contrast, other traditions share the belief that the body is a prison of the Soul and therefore needs to be liberated so it can continue on its journey toward enlightenment. Obviously, in these traditions, I'm not only a welcome guest but an honored guest because My job is essential to continued growth.

Others see Me as the "messenger of joy" for the person who has died, ready to take that Soul on a spiritual adventure.

In contrast to these positive views of who I am, there are others that believe I represent the continued punishment of mankind for its rebellion against God. Therefore, by their standards, I'm seen as negative, the opposite of purity, life, light, and eternal salvation for the dead person.

I have purposefully not labeled which traditions belong to which current religion so as not to insult any reader. Again, you the reader knows your particular religious' beliefs and how they relate to Me. It is now up to you to decide whether you continue to believe those traditions or believe what I am telling you here.

If I could choose how I'd like to be perceived, I'd come to humanity as a floating warm orb of light pulsating like a heartbeat and a voice understood by all. This would show everyone that I'm part of the Eternal, Universal Life Force that allows the Soul to achieve new experiences for further growth and understanding to become ever closer to the Higher Source.

Just like the Higher Source, I'm not one Being; I can't show "My face" or become human-like to demonstrate My benign semblance. I am everywhere because I am Light.

Chapter 2: Death is the New Beginning

Question: When the Soul is released, is this truly a new beginning? Also, please talk about ghosts, specters, and people who are able to communicate with departed souls.

Answer:

Death of the physical body represents the opportunity for each Soul to grow and draw closer to the Light and Wisdom of the Universe. Only through the liberation of the Soul from the physical body is it possible for that Soul to achieve new heights (no pun intended)!

It's certainly easy to understand why death is seen as final. Your logical brain uses five senses to understand the physical world around you. These are the only channels of perception available to most humans. Yes, there are those who are blind or deaf or both, but in these individuals, the other senses develop a heightened awareness to compensate. So, you can clearly understand that these five senses can only explore the physical world. That's their limited capability.

Imagine, instead, that humans have many other senses that can tap into and experience a world that isn't physical as humans know it. This world does exist, and people who have either a natural ability to use these extra senses or those who learn to use them can apprehend and interact with this non-physical world. Many of you scoff at people who say they can see and talk to the dead, are aware of ghosts, or are able to connect with those who've died. As in all things, there are charlatans who want to take your money or people who simply want others to feel less sad, so they make up stories about those who have passed. However, there are those among you who truly can connect with those who've died. How is that possible, you ask, if I've taken their Souls elsewhere? I'm Light and therefore everywhere, and when a Soul is no longer restrained by a physical body, it's everywhere too.

I know this is a difficult concept for many of you to understand, because you're so connected to that physical body, but think for a moment. A Soul is part of the greater Light of the Universe. A Soul can be everywhere, just as Light is, because it's part of that Light. Therefore, yes, it's possible to communicate with that Soul if you have the ability to do so. In fact, that Soul has the ability to "appear" to you in the form of its physical manifestation in its previous life, so you can recognize it. Your brain, with its five senses, has a difficult time acknowledging anything outside its usual perceptions, so that Soul must present itself to you as you once knew it in it's physical form, to be recognized.

You also asked "What about ghosts? Why, if a person's Soul has passed to another plane, might it persist on earth in the form of a ghost"? Again, that Soul is everywhere. As it heals itself, it may choose to do that healing here on earth. Healing doesn't mean the Soul needs to re-enter another body and take a physical form. Nor does it mean the Soul must take another form in another plane. It can persist here on earth, as a Soul, to repair itself.

There are Souls that find it difficult to figure out how to repair themselves. I can't help them in this effort. These Souls must find their own way. I'm only with them to show them the Light and how they're part of it. They eventually work out their healing for themselves, in "their" time, which takes only an instant. In your time, it can be many generations.

You might also wonder about specters, those beings that bring terror and sometimes inhabit another's body. Are they real? Yes, specters are, most unfortunately, real. Souls take this form because of their refusal to come with Me to the place of Light and Understanding.

A Soul that has lived within a human body, has free choice. This isn't lost when the body dies. In fact, free choice is part of the Soul, not the physical body. Most Souls come with Me joyfully on the journey to a place of rest and restoration, a place where the next learning adventure presents itself. However, there are some

Souls who refuse to come with Me. I can't command any Soul to do My bidding or accompany Me. It's their choice. Some are so desperate to return to their old human existence that instead of joining Me to start the work of healing they prefer to stay in the physical realm where there body once resided. These are Souls that have usually experienced a traumatic, untimely death and have not processed completely what has happened to them nor have they felt they were given the opportunity to say their goodbyes properly. Eventually, they will accept their fate and move onward with Me, towards the healing they need.

But let me be clear: The Souls of those you love and who love you are always with you, not in the sense that they are inside you, but with you in Spirit. That also doesn't mean they're stuck on earth. As Light, Souls can be anywhere and everywhere. Therefore, Souls will strive to be with their human family whenever they're needed, even though they're also in another plane on their own journey.

Chapter 3: The Death of Pets

Question: What about the death of our pets?

Answer:

Ah…I'd be remiss not to talk to you about your pets. Those of you who've loved an animal as part of your family have infused that animal with a special human gift that only you are allowed to give to other living things. This gift involves transferring to that animal a part of your Soul. The Love you give transcends the physical realm and allows an animal, your pet, to become part of your Soul. As such, when this beloved member of your family dies, its Soul is allowed to return to the owner and thus the two remain together. If there have been several owners, the Soul returns to all who loved this animal. Like Light, the animal's Soul can exist with many.

Those who "see" their pet after it passes aren't imagining things. That Soul is Love, and Love can show itself in different ways. If the pet doesn't present itself to you in physical form, that doesn't mean the pet loved you any less. Remember our discussion of those who have senses capable of feeling or "seeing" a Soul? The same applies to feeling the presence of or seeing your pet that's died. If this sense is developed, you're more apt to be given the gift of visiting with your departed pet. However, please understand that when you pass, your Soul is forever reunited with your beloved pet or pets.

What about the Souls of wild animals, or animals that humans eat? Just as humans have been given the special gift of transferring part of their Soul to animals they love, wild animals or those consumed for food are loved by the Universe and, as such, have a special place within the realm of Light and Love. Although these living beings don't have a human-like Soul, as part of the Universe, they're intensely loved. Otherwise, why would they have been saved in the Great Flood? What would it matter?

I might add that Native Americans have a beautiful tradition of linking an animal spirit with that of a human. For instance, someone in the tribe may be linked to the wolf, another to the eagle, and so forth. This concept helps explain what I've described above, which is the essence of animals and their relationship to the Universe. That essence, although not a Soul, is sacred to the Universe. That essence, according to Native American traditions, can link to a human's Soul to guide that Soul during life on earth.

So, then, what does it mean when these animals die? If they have no Souls, do they simply disappear? Remember, "Energy can't be created nor destroyed," to quote Albert Einstein, and the Soul is energy. Therefore, no, they don't disappear. Yes, their physical body returns to the earth, but their essence, as part of the Universe, remains within the realm of Love and Light. Collectively, they return to the Light of the Universe and continues to power it. Imagine how it would be if the Light that's given to all living things died with them. If their Light, their energy, didn't return to the Universe, the Universe would slowly dim until it no longer existed. That, of course, will never happen.

How can you know that what I tell you is true? Recall the photographs that claim to show the auras of living things. Many believe such photographs have been thoroughly debunked through scientific experiments. However, science has yet to prove My existence, the existence of the Godhead, the Creator of All, or the existence of anything unable to be perceived by the five senses. Therefore, you must admit that science isn't able to answer all questions. If it were, there would be cures for all diseases. Why does science fail? It fails because it can only rely on the physical world as represented by the five senses. The greatest, most powerful telescope, microscope, or accelerator is simply an extension of these five senses.

Therefore, just as you can't discredit Me because I can't be quantified, you can't discredit that living things contain an essence that appears as an aura. All living things have an essence that's transferred as Light to the

Universe on their passing. The essence of Souls is Light, and this Light also reunites with the Universe, as we've discussed, but in a different manner. Each Soul retains its individual Light as it unites with the Universe's collective Light. Imagine a bunch of candles, each with its own light but contributing to the collective light. The same pertains to the Light within Souls, which retain their individuality but contribute to the total Light of the Universe.

EPILOGUE

Life on this earth is complicated. Relationships between humans, between humans and animals, and between humans and all living things are complicated on so many levels.

As complicated as life is, My presence hasn't brought humans to a better understanding of the bigger picture, so to speak. The common fear is that the end of physical life is the end of everything. I hope My answers to the questions posed during this intimate interview have helped diminish this fear.

I agreed to be interviewed so I could tell My side of the story in the hope you'll finally let go of fear and realize the truth of My being—I'm Light, and the gentle partner of the Godhead, the Universe, the All Knowing.

FINAL THOUGHTS

I stated before, that I would review the "commandments", the basic human beliefs of correct behavior while on earth as given to you by the Higher Source. These interpretations will then be My final gifts to you so that you can better understand that there is a "higher" interpretation of the "laws" as put forth by the Universe. As I write these out for you, the I and Me below, refers to the Higher Source, the All Knowing, whatever name you wish to give the Giver of All Life. It does not refer to Me, Death. Open your mind and let your Soul help your mind understand these truths. Through these interpretations, My hope is that your Soul may travel with more ease through the earthly physical existence and the hardships it faces, in preparation for your journey with Me.

During these very trying times in your physical world, remember that I will be with you when your time is near to travel with Me. When you see the end coming for someone you love or for yourself, always remember this: I am Light, I am comfort, I am the gentle breeze that will take hold of your Soul and carry it on My wings to unimaginable Warmth and Love. I'll carry you to rejoin the Light of the Universe and there you'll reunite with the Souls with whom you share an eternal destiny.

Heed My words and never fear, for I am near

THE UNIVERSAL LAWS

Within the parenthesis, is the law as humans know it. What follows is the interpretation by the Universe, with an explanation.

Law #1: (*I am the Lord thy God*). I am the Alpha and the Omega, the Beginning and the End, the All-Knowing, Universal Love.

Your Soul, as all Souls do, inherently understands that it is part of a greater Source of Love and Knowledge. It understands that it cannot exist within a vacuum and is an equally important part of the Whole.

Law#2: (*You shall have no other god images*). I am the Universe, the Everything.

There are no other greater Sources of Knowledge, Love or All Knowing. I am the Beginning and the End, the Eternal and no other is greater than the Higher Source of All. There is no image possible to represent the Higher Source, because I am Light, Love and Am everywhere.

Law #3: (*You shall not use My name in vain*). Respect the Higher Source, Creator of All

As the Source of All, I must be respected always. To think or believe I am anything less than what I am is inherently counter-intuitive to your origin.

Law #4: (*Remember to keep the Sabbath*) Rest your Soul from the daily grind

Never take for granted the wonder of your Soul as part of this Universe and allow it to rest and understand the beauty of this concept. Enjoy each breath given to you by the Higher Source. By doing so, your Soul will honor the Universe and the Creator of All. Remember, Life is but a Breath, a Holy Breath.

Law#5: (*Honor your mother and your father*) Souls must acknowledge and respect their origin and their part of a greater Whole.

The human law of honoring your mother and father is not meant to be taken literally, but instead must be understood as the inherent quality each Soul possesses of belonging to the Creator of All, of which you are, so to speak Its children. Although to acknowledge those who have given you human life is important, to take this literally would, for example, place those whose mothers and fathers abused them, as above the law of the Universe.

Law #6: (*You shall not kill*) Do not take a Soul's physical body for malicious intent.

Remember that each Soul has the inherent right to exist within the Universe and as such cannot take another Soul. The law has been interpreted literally to mean a human cannot kill another human. However, as it has been explained before, taking a life can only be considered killing when it is done with malicious intent, not to liberate from suffering.

Law#7: (*You shall not commit adultery*) Do not attempt to unite with another Soul on the basis of wanting that Soul.

Each Soul belongs to a particular body. Do not attempt to unite with that body, if it does not belong to you, among the confines of human law and decency.

Law #8: (*You shall not steal*) Do not take from the Universe, what is not yours to take.

The Universe gives you an abundance of opportunities to improve the world around you. Do not make that world less perfect by taking what does not belong to you.
.
Law #9: (*You shall not lie*) The Higher Source knows all and knows the lies you tell yourselves and others.

Your Souls will always know the truth. Do not taint the Soul with untruths that it has to try to defend.

Law# 10: (*You shall not want what others have*) The Universe has given you everything you need in this life to continue to repair your Souls and learn.

Do not want what you do not need to improve your Soul. Any excess will not help your Soul grow and move forward towards Me, the Creator.

ABOUT THE AUTHOR

Cristina Carballo-Perelman, M.D. has been a physician for over 30 years, providing care and comfort to many of her patients as they take their last breath.

She has struggled throughout her career with Death, as the persona that represents finality. Because of this struggle, Death has asked her to help explain to the world how humanity should view Death, not with fear but with the hope for a new life. Because she has seen this fear in her patient's families, she agreed to give Death a voice, a platform to explain Itself.

This book is, therefore meant to comfort both the individual facing death and help their loved one's cope.
For those facing their or a loved one's mortality, she also recommends the companion book she has written, *Hush Dear Soul, Your Time is Near, A Lullaby for the Soul.*

The author lives in Scottsdale, AZ with her husband and two dogs.

www.ingramcontent.com/pod-product-compliance
Lightning Source LLC
Chambersburg PA
CBHW052131010526
44113CB00034B/1672